Your Black & White Family Wild Arts Activities

Volume I

Strengthening Family Through Nature - based Creativity

Kim Nunneley

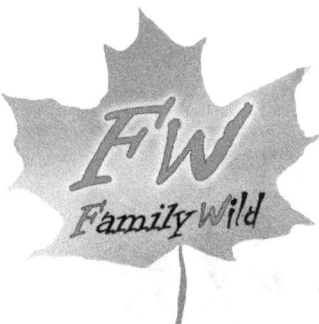

Family Wild Club Registration

Register Your Club for free at:
www.familywildprogram.com
on the Contact Page

Give your club a name like <u>Nunneley Family Wild</u> register it to join the *Family Wild Nation!*

Family Wild

"It is never too late to be what you might have been."

— George Elliot

Family Wild

"Keep your love of nature, for that is the true way to understand art more and more."

Artist - Vincent Van Gogh

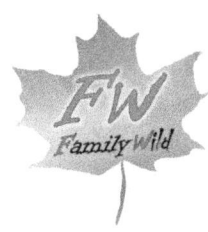 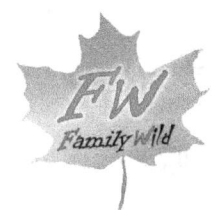

Family Wild Library

Your Family Wild Hunting Club Manual
Your Family Wild Fishing Club Manual
Your Family Wild Arts Club Manual

Your Family Wild Hunting SLAM Journal
Your Family Wild Fishing SLAM Journal
Your Family Wild Arts SLAM Journal

Your Family Wild Hunting Activities Handbook-Volume I
Your Family Wild Fishing Activities Handbook-Volume I
Your Family Wild Arts Activities Handbook-Volume I

Your Family Wild Annual Hunting Record Book
Your Family Wild Annual Fishing Record Book

Your Family Wild ALL-TIME Hunting Record Book
Your Family Wild ALL-TIME Fishing Record Book

Coming Soon!
Your Family Wild Hunting Coloring Book
Your Family Wild Fishing Coloring Book
Your Family Wild Photography Book
Your Family Wild Deer Blind Journal
Your Family Wild Hunting Camp Journal
Your Family Wild Fishing Journal
Your Family Wild White-Tail Deer Harvest Journal

Copyright © 2017 by Kim Nunneley & Family Wild, LLC

All rights reserved. No part of this publication may be reproduced, distributed, or transmitted in any form or by any means, including photocopying, recording, or other electronic or mechanical methods, without the prior written permission of the publisher, except in the case of brief quotations embodied in critical reviews and certain other noncommercial uses permitted by copyright law. For permission requests, email to the publisher, addressed "Attention: Permissions Coordinator," at the email address below.

Family Wild, LLC
Email address: famiywild@familywildprogram.com

Website: www.familywild.com
Facebook-https://www.facebook.com/Familywild2016/

Family Wild Online Store - **www.familywildprogram.com**

The information provided within this Book is for general informational purposes only. While we try to keep the information up-to-date and correct, there are no representations or warranties, express or implied, about the completeness, accuracy, reliability, suitability or availability with respect to the information, products, services, or related graphics contained in this Book for any purpose. Any use of this information is at your own risk and the risk of your friends and family.

The information contained within this Book is strictly for educational purposes. If you wish to apply ideas contained in this Book, you are taking full responsibility for your actions.

ISBN-13: 9781976501968

Cover Illustration Copyright © 2017 M W Nunneley
Cover design by M W Nunneley
Editing by Kim Nunneley
Author photograph by Del Beyer & M.W. Nunneley

Family Wild

> "He KNOWS and that makes me Happy every day!"
>
> Kim Nunneley
> **Author**

Family Wild

"Look deep into nature, and then you will understand everything better."

Albert Einstein

Acknowledgements

From Kim: This work, which is part of the Family Wild series of books, wholly captured my imagination. I have to thank the people who instilled in me a deep appreciation for all things "wild and wonderful"-

My father for his love of fishing;

My mother for her boundless enthusiasm for birds at the feeder;

My grandfather who taught me to sit on logs and just listen;

My grandmother who canned and preserved and gardened in the hot Indiana sunshine;

My brother who considers the cathedral of the forest his church;

My stepdaughter for throwing off the "girl" stereotypes as she hunts and fishes;

My son who faints at the sight of his own blood but happily digs into fish and squirrel cleaning;

The many horses of my life who went where my short legs and asthma-prone body could not, meandering down foggy trails that smelled of pine and earth;

Poets like Mary Oliver and Wendell Berry who celebrate Creation in their juicy and inviting ways;

My husband who is so enthusiastically committed to helping families find each other again through hunting, fishing and the arts;

To these and so many more, my deepest bow of thanks for the gift of learning to dance with the natural world!

Family Wild

> *"Never forget the trail, look ever for the track in the snow; it is the priceless, unimpeachable record of the creature's life and thought, in the oldest writing known on the earth."*
>
> Ernest Thompson Seton
> (from *Mammal Tracks and Sign*)

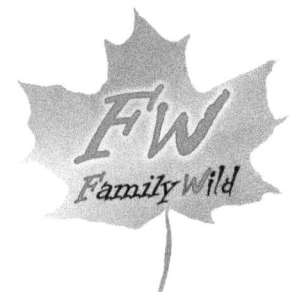
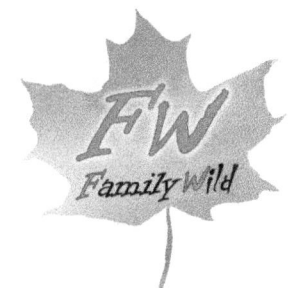

Your Black & White
Family Wild
Art Activities

Table of Contents

Acknowledgments	9
1. Welcome	**13**
2. Activity Submission	**17**
3. Arts Activities	**25**
Gardening for the Hunt	27
Bird Feeding Stations	31
Simple Bird Treats	37
Recipes and Recipe Book	41
Dehydrator Fun	47
Pressing Flowers	51
Hunting/Fishing Journals	59
Poetry and Nature	65
Wildlife Journalism	71
Personalize your Life Preserver	77
Music in the Wild	81
Painting Wildlife	85
Drawing Wildlife	89
Sculpting Wildlife	95
Wildlife Photography	101
Blogs and Facebook	105
Outdoor Comic Design	111
Tanning Hides	119
Wildlife Taxidermy	127
Capturing Animal Tracks	133
Worm Composter	137
Hatching a Butterfly	143
Creating a Fish Scaler	149
Night Crawler Ninja	153
Animal Cleaning Station	157
Fish Cleaning Station	163
4. Highest Honor	**169**
Appendix	**179**
Adult Photo Release	181
Child Photo Release	182
Intellectual Release	183
FW Vision Statement	184
FW Mission Statement	185
Family Wild Website	186
About the Author	187

Family Wild

"I am always doing that which I cannot do, in order that I may learn how to do it."

Pablo Picasso

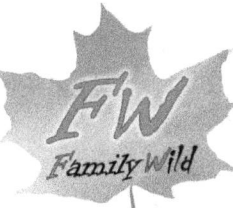 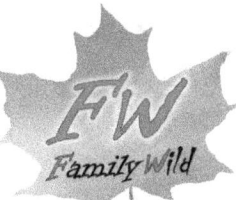

1
Welcome

Wild QUOTE

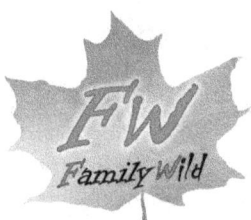 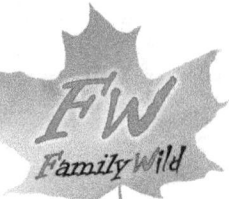

Family Wild Motto

"Hunting, Fishing, Loving Every Day."

Luke Bryan

Country Singer

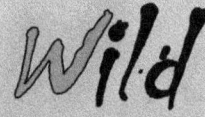

QUOTE

"Habitat for wildlife is continually shrinking - I can at least provide a way station."

Peter Coyote

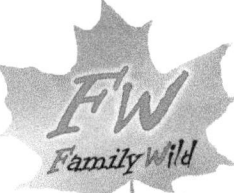 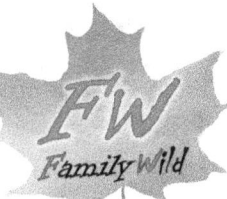

Welcome
Objective-Get Family Wild!

Family Wild sprang to life in 2016 as a way to connect family members to each other through the nature sports of hunting and fishing, as well as the arts that call us to interact with all things wild. This book shows you how to create your own Family Wild club!

Creating your own Family Wild encourages YOUR family - children, teens, parents, grandparents - the entire unit of family and friends - to gather regularly to create and celebrate the natural environment through activities, images, words, delicious food, and the construction of practical hunting aids.

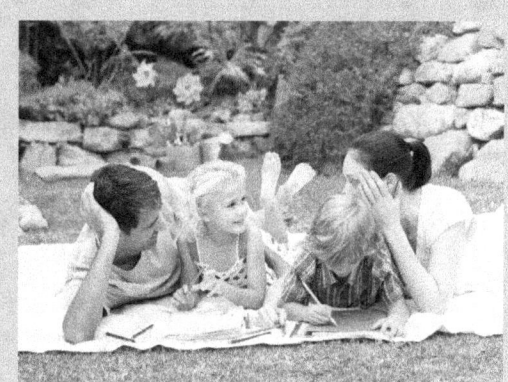

Family Wild emphasizes families and friends **DOING THINGS TOGETHER IN NATURE.** The more you take this to heart, the richer your Family Wild experience!

We encourage children, teens and adults to log their accomplishments and strive to earn "Grand Slam" achievement certificates. Visit the FW webpage at **www.familywildprogram.com** to view the Grand Slam Achievement certificates and plaques and follow the directions to order your award to show off your family's accomplishments!

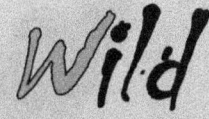

"I feel like I'm nothing without wildlife. They are the stars. I feel awkward without them."

Bindi Irwin

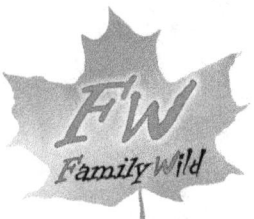
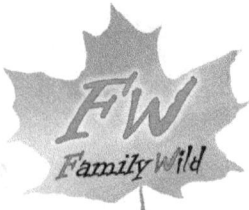

Welcome

We've filled the Family Wild Library of books with great activities and projects for your entire family.

Further, we offer you FREE additional programing at the Family Wild website and blog. This allows us to point you and your family to the very best educational sources available and helps to expand the scope of your fun.

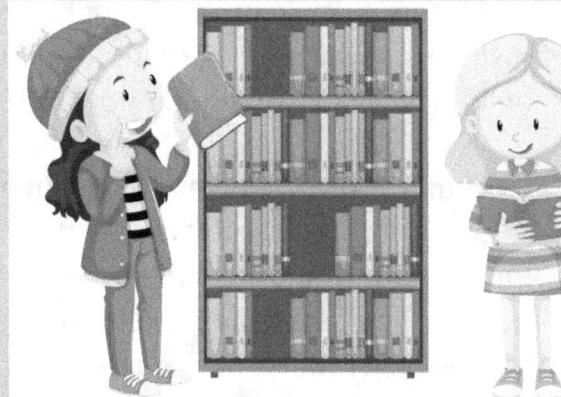

We've tried to keep our activities relatively low cost and family friendly. Allow your children to do as much as they can on their own - don't let your own expectations limit their resourcefulness! Given the opportunity, your children will stun you with what they can actually accomplish when they set their minds to it!

"I recall watching my son, an avowed computer geek, build his first 2x4 wall and clean his first squirrel - only then did I realize his abilities far exceeded my expectations!"   *- Kim Nunneley*

When you do need to step in and help, remember to keep a sense of humor and play. Dare to **CREATE** precious and fun-filled *Family Wild* memories **TOGETHER!**

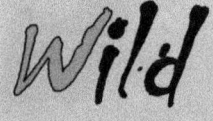

QUOTE

"Plans to protect air and water, wilderness and wildlife are in fact plans to protect man."

Stewart Udall

Visit us at www.familywildprogram.com

Like us on Facebook at Family Wild

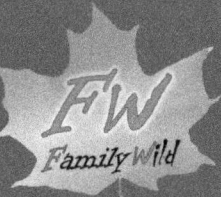

Family Wild

Chapter 2 Activity Submissions

Family Wild Activities

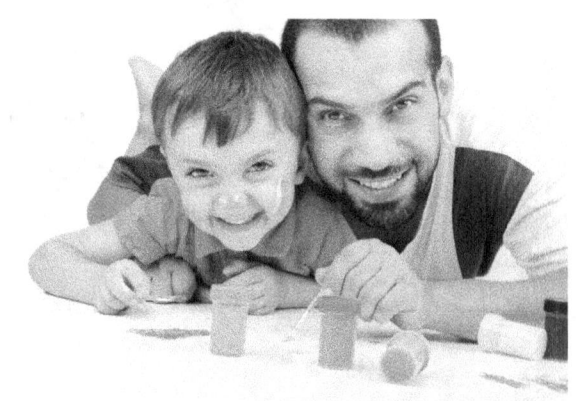

Throughout this section, we'll give you a taste of our *Family Wild* **Activities Books.** Our activities collection is a continuing series of publications offering you a variety of projects and group fun for your *Family Wild* club.

While tournaments may occur monthly or one weekend during a particular hunting or fishing season, you can enjoy activities after work, during school vacations, or even on weekends.

IMPORTANT ANNOUNCEMENT
FAMILY WILD needs <u>YOUR</u> help.

Although we have a bunch of great ideas for activities, we know we don't have them all. So, we want you to submit your ideas and pictures of you doing your activities to us at *Family Wild*.

We want art, hunting or fishing activities, no matter how big or small, simple or complicated. We also want ideas for fishing and hunting themes that incorporate writing, painting, photography, sculpture, videography, gardening, recipes and cooking or construction like blinds and bird feeders.

Family Wild will then go through the submissions to pick the very best ideas for our next release. If we select yours, we'll send you a complimentary edition!

Look for additional information later in this book or visit our website at **www.familywildprogram.com** for details about how to make your activity and family famous in future *Family Wild* publications.

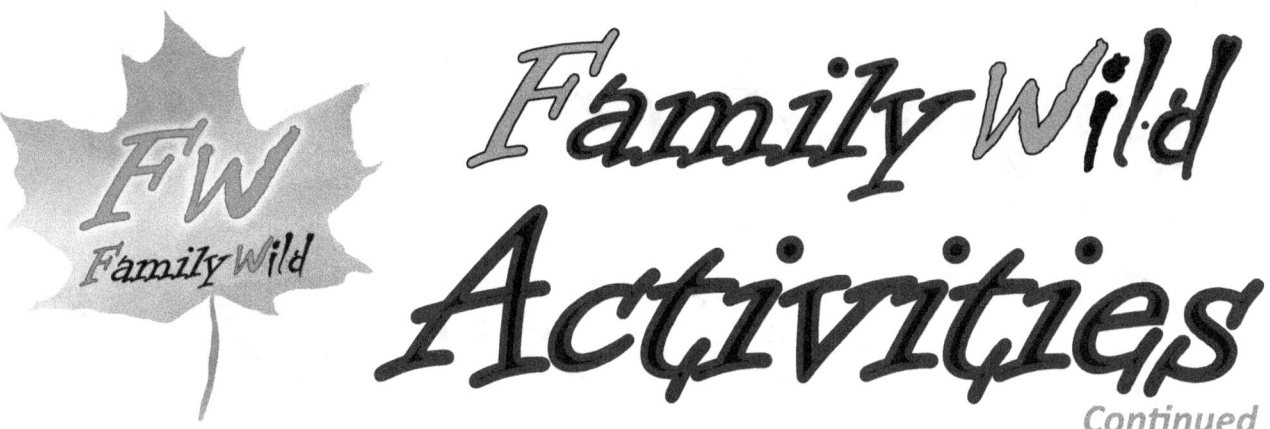

Family Wild Activities *Continued*

At **Family Wild**, we love hearing the story behind your activity. As a result, we ask that you give us the fun details of the activity. You also may want to give your activity to someone outside of your family to review or try to make sure you've made it "doable" for someone unfamiliar with your type of hunting, fishing or art. Keep in mind, we target both world class folks as well as young beginners with our activities.

Ask yourself the following questions when you summarize your activity:

Who can do this activity? Is there an age group that should do this or, more importantly, shouldn't? Should parts of this project be done by an adult?

What is the activity? What supplies do you need? What tools? What part of the activity is more child-friendly? What challenges may arise? What safety concerns should you consider?

How long will this activity take? Can you accomplish this in minutes, hours, or do you need a weekend or longer?

Where should this activity occur? Should part of it be done at home or camp and the other in the field or on the lake?

Why would you want to try this activity? What are your goals for everyone who attempts this?

How do you go about preparing for this activity? How do you begin?

Finally, and in our opinion, most important, tell us the "family story" behind your activity. Who taught you or who have you taught? Tell us the history: the good, the bad, the ugly and the funny.

Please include pictures of your family doing the activity. Remember, you'll need to complete our Photo Releases for all adults and children (found in the Appendix or our website **www.familywildprogram.com.**) Also fill out the Activity Cover Sheet as well as the Intellectual Property Release.

With a little luck, we'll publish YOUR FAMILY'S experience in our next activity book and, if we do, we'll send you a free copy as our thank you.

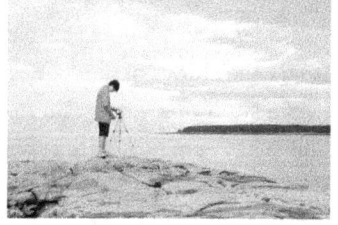

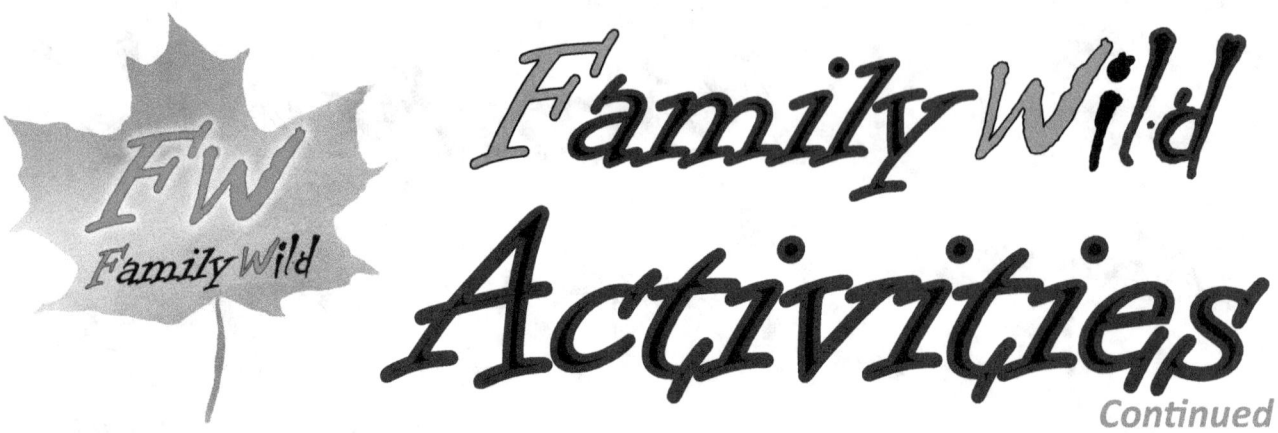

Family Wild Activities
Continued

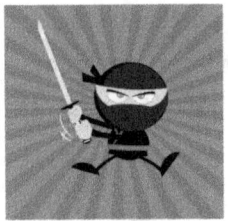

The **Family Wild** Activity Series of Books came from night crawler picking of all things. My Grandmother (yes, Grandmother) taught all of her grandchildren how to pick crawlers and worms at night after a summer rain.

Imagine a four-foot, eleven-inch tall Night Crawler Ninja stalking like a preying mantis, flashlight in one hand and fingers near the ground with the other, waiting to cobra strike the unsuspecting fish bait.

All the grandchildren learned that Grandma and Grandpa had a small gas station and bait shop on Long Lake. They picked crawlers to sell to put money in the till and food on the table. At sixty years old, Grandma ended up teaching a gaggle of grandkids the all-but-lost art of hunting their own fishing bait as well as a family tradition we all still laugh about when we remember Grandma.

Flash forward 40 years. I took my new wife, Kim, and step-son, Ian, crawler picking. As we jumped out of the car with flashlights in hand, they both proceeded to stomp through the yard like two Transformers headed to battle. "STOP!" I begged. They both looked at me puzzled and confused.

As I worked my way in front of them, I immediately went into our family's traditional Night Crawler Ninja position. As I crept forward, light shining the ground for the little crawlers, I heard giggles behind me. My loving wife and step-son couldn't contain themselves at the presence of the six-foot tall, 299.5 pound, Night Crawler Ninja.

Now I must admit, given my sense of humor, I understood how they may have concluded they had boarded another Michael practical joke bus, fully equipped with lights and buckets, in search of giant night crawlers. They both sounded as if they knew the punch line to the joke and couldn't contain themselves, until...

...the FLASH of the Night Crawler Ninja's right hand plucked an unsuspecting giant worm from its hole in the ground. Suddenly silence replaced giggles as they watched the struggle between hunter and hunted. Success!!!

A few minutes later, Kim and Ian joined generations of my family as they prowled the back yard for the next day's fishing bait. Although neither met the Ninja Sensei, they both learned a craft that started for me and my family with Grandma Marie, the original Night Crawler Ninja Warrior.

Thus began what would become the **Family Wild** Activities model. In our activity books, we want to share the stories of outdoor activities you've learned from your grandparents, parents, family or friends. More importantly, we want to encourage you to pass these traditions on to your children/grandchildren and allow **Family Wild** to share them with other members.

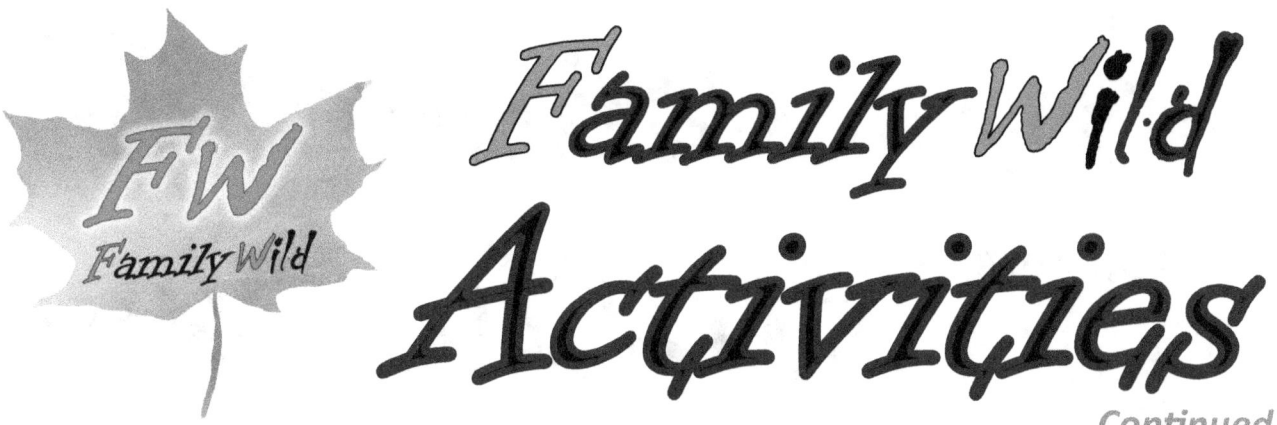

Family Wild Activities
Continued

Hunters, fisherman and artist all come with a bag of tricks they guarantee will help you bag a bigger buck, grab your limit or create something astonishing. If you want to watch an old outdoorsman's or artist eyes beam, ask them how they hunt for this, fish for that, or create their craft and then grab a chair and get comfortable.

Sometimes, you just learn things in the moment. For example, my Grandfather Ken told me you always troll walleyes with 100 feet of line and a Rapala lure behind the pontoon. I still clean rabbits the way my Grandpa Cranston showed me how to do as a teenager. To this day, I still compare every jar of homemade strawberry jelly to my Grandma Gertrude's. Oh, I forgot to mention, the Night Crawler Ninja, Grandma Marie, also showed me the patience of unscrambling the fishing line tangle, otherwise known as a "nest-mess."

Please don't think we won't find your activity interesting or worthy of publishing. In most cases, we may find the story behind the activity actually determines what we publish.

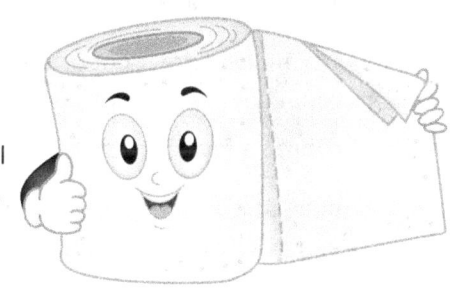

Let me give you an example. After I shot my first buck as a 16 year-old, I ran (picture the Stay Puff Marshmallow Man in hunter orange) to camp to get my Uncle Gary to help me track my deer. As I entered the camp huffing and puffing, I stammered that I'd shot a buck.

My uncle calmly grabbed my gun and made sure I'd engaged the safety. I hadn't because my gun jammed in my hurry to "rack" another round (young hunters - **DON'T DO THIS!!!** Make sure you've put the safety on every time unless you plan to shoot again. Adults, always check this with your young hunters, especially if they're excited in the moment).

Then my Uncle Gary told me to do the darndest thing I'd ever heard. He told me to get a roll of toilet paper. Dumbfounded, I literally replied "I didn't mess my pants and I don't need to go to the bathroom." He laughed and told me we would use the sheets of toilet paper to mark the blood stains on the leaf covered autumn ground. The white toilet paper would allow us to relocate the blood trail, should we lose it.

This is just one example of a wisdom - nugget I've never forgotten and will pass on to the next generation of Nunneley *Family Wild* hunters.

Family Wild Activities

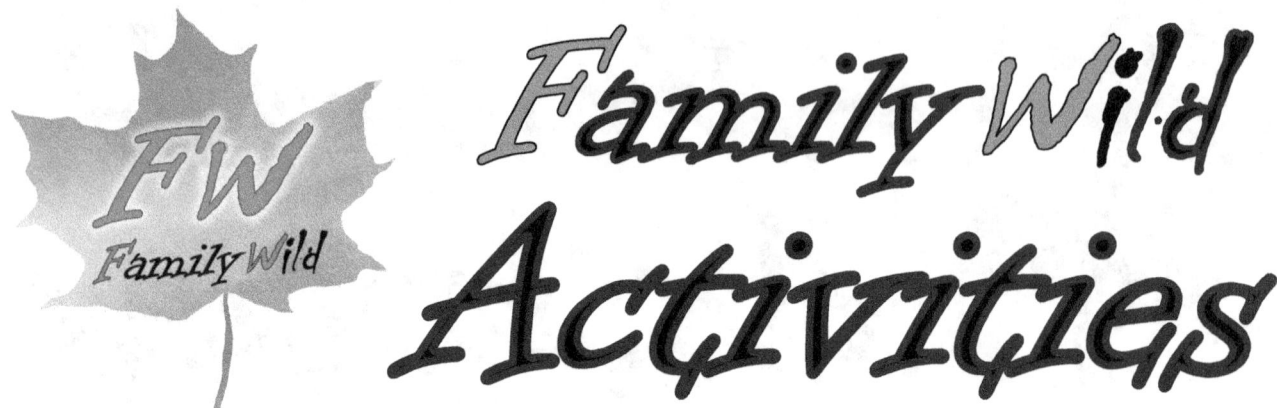

Continued

At **Family Wild**, we've tried to include options and activities for everyone. Maybe your spouse doesn't enjoy hunting or fishing. Maybe your middle child lives for the woods but doesn't care for fishing. On the other hand, your oldest loves photography or videography but doesn't like to hunt. Bringing up the rear, your youngest loves to go to camp and loves to sit in the blind but hates anything icky.

As a result, we want to offer activities for everyone. Maybe your family goes for long rides looking for wildlife and you keep a camera in the car to "hunt" that Bald Eagle or Snowy Owl. Perhaps your youngest always writes in their journal about your day at camp. What if your spouse paints a bird scene? All of these activities could find their way into our next activity book. Just make sure to highlight your **Family Wild** STORY along with the activity.

Looking for another great opportunity for you to pass on your tradition? Send us your FAMOUS wildlife-based recipes. Of course, we want mouth-watering meals from the field *and* the store. You don't have to kill it to submit a favorite dish for the **Family Wild** Recipes Book.

For example, at our camp, Coach always whipped up a venison meal that left everyone 10 pounds heavier and EVERY DISH DIRTIED IN THE CAMP. The "kids" didn't want dish detail when Coach took over the kitchen. The fun of this camp story was the mountain of dirty dishes that appeared year after year.

Another example would be my "world famous" Chili. I call it the my Clean Out The Kitchen Chili. First, I buy one can of every type of bean or bean-like thing in the store. Then, I go up and down the aisle searching for anything that may work in my concoction. Every year, there has to be one thing I've never included before. This is how Nestle's Chocolate and peanut butter have both found their ways into my creation. I always put in 2 pounds of ground venison. Finally, the determining factor to see if it's done? I check to see if a soup ladle stands straight up in the middle of it. Every family has that story that surrounds a special meal. Put yours into 400-500 words along with the recipe and see if makes our upcoming **Family Wild** *Recipe Guide*. Again, if your entry makes the book, we'll send you a free copy as our thank you. Submit to

FamilyWild@familywildprogram.com

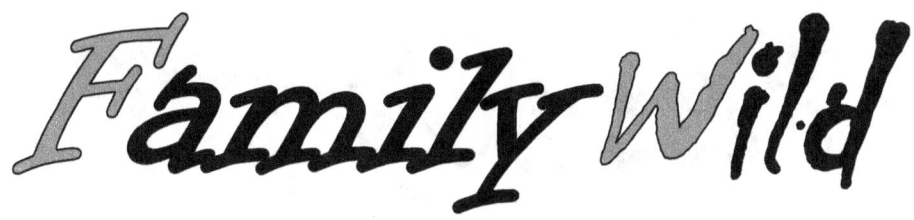

Family Wild Activity

Application Form

Applicant Name _____

Address _____

Phone # _____

Email Address _____

Activity Name _____

Items Included with Application

____ Application Description (400-500 words)

____ Application Story (400-500 words)

____ Activity Photos (1-3 photos)

____ Adult Photo Releases - Signed

____ Children Photo Releases Signed

____ Intellectual Property Release - Signed

EMAIL US YOUR ACTIVITY THROUGH OUR WEBSITE

Family Wild

> "Don't cry because it's over, smile because it happened."
>
> — Dr. Seuss

Visit us at www.familywildprogram.com

Like us on Facebook at Family Wild

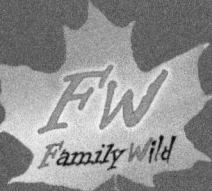

Family Wild

Chapter 3
Arts Activities

Family Wild

"At first they'll ask you why you're doing it. But then they'll ask you how you did it."

Author Unknown

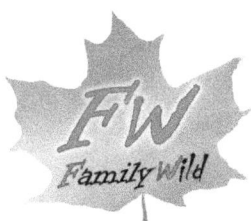
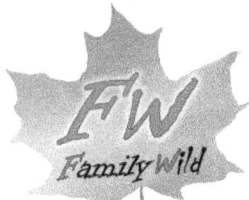

Gardening for the Hunt

Deer and Small Game Plots

Objective: Design a simple garden with features that will draw in game animals or wildlife to enjoy.

What You Might Need:

Graph paper and pen

Rototiller

Shovel

Seed broadcaster

Access to shrubs

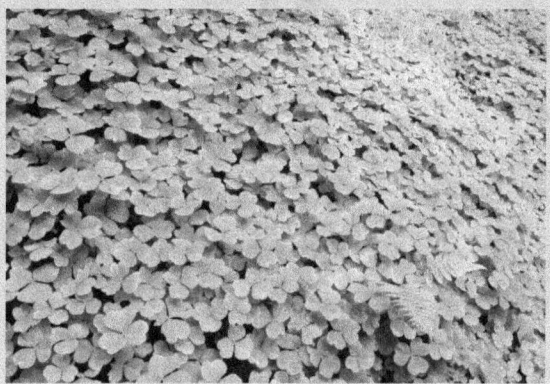

Access to loose branches

Small pond or birdbath

Corn seeds

Sunflower seeds

Winter grain seeds

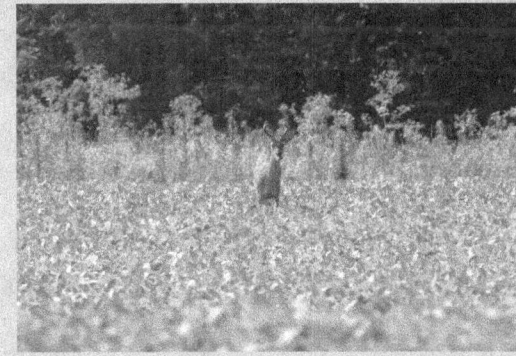

Jump in!

Wild QUOTE

"The artist and the photographer seek the mysteries and the adventure of experience in nature."

Ansel Adams - Photographer

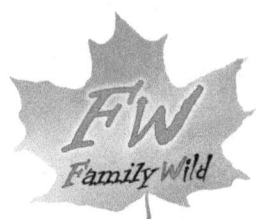

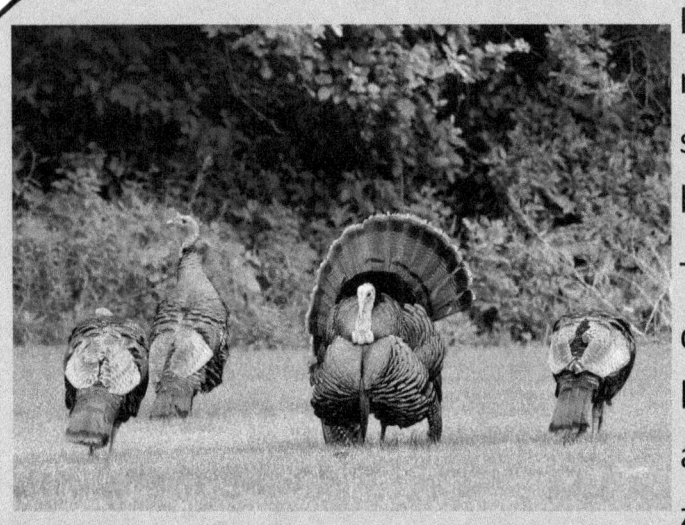

Remember to leave enough room for shelter-birdhouses, squirrel houses, bat boxes, brush piles and the like.

The more careful planning you do, the better your results will be. Take time to choose seeds and plants for your growing zone and learn about how to care for them-how much sun do they need? Do they require supplemental soil building? How much water do they require?

When you have done all your research and are read to "dig in", try to break the task down into small work-day bites:

Stake out your area with twine and wooden stakes
Prepare the soil
Select your seeds and plants and prep them for transfer into your new plot
Planting and watering day

Remember, you can often rent rototillers - they are very helpful for breaking up raw ground. Gardening implements are good garage sale finds or Craig's list fodder - you don't have to invest a ton upfront.

Have fun inviting the Wild home!

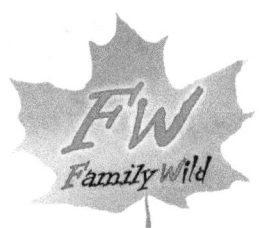

If you are lucky enough to have a large yard or acreage, you may be able to create shelter, food plots and watering holes that will draw in wildlife. Generally, there are three things to keep in mind:

Animals need shelter. For small game, that means brush piles. For birds, tall grasses and trees; for deer, areas of dense browsing height trees or areas to bed down in when winter comes. Animals need food. Check out your state's DNR website to learn what kind of plants, both domesticated and wild, will draw in the animal you most want. Animals need water. Adding a small pond or even birdbaths to your garden plan will help keep animals close by.

Take some time to decide what kinds of animals you want to invite in. For instance, if you are in an urban setting, you might just want to create a wild bird sanctuary. If you have enough land to hunt, you can take advantage of your space to create feed plots and shelter for a variety of animals.

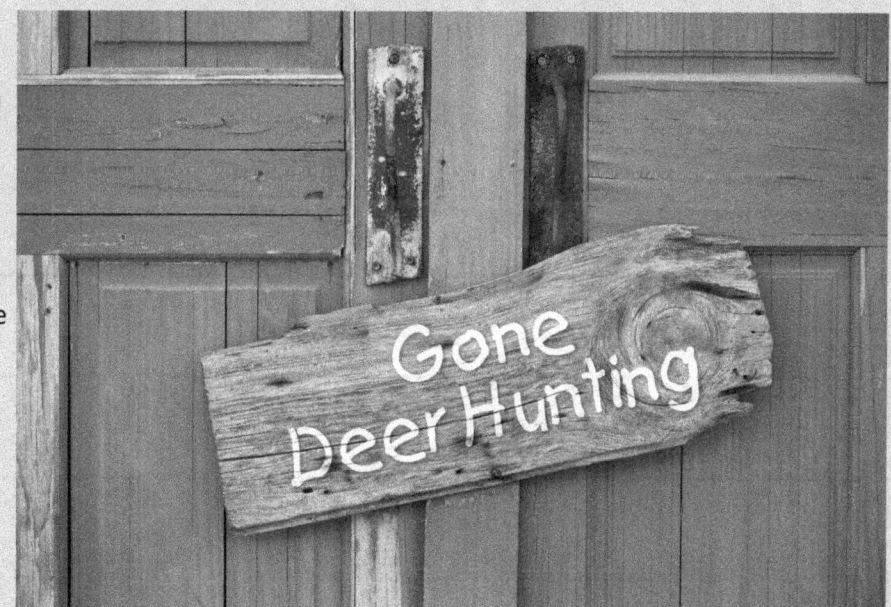

Take your graph paper and sketch in your home, barns, or other structures. Then, search the web under "hunting food plots" or by your favorite animal. Some sites have pre-planned gardens you can easily duplicate on your own land.

Often contacting your local county extension office will point you to a huge storehouse of information about garden layout and even what kinds of seeds and plants will do best in your area.

SCRAPBOOK PICTURES

Glue a couple pictures here
to remember your Activity

You can keep the pictures in Your Family Wild Activity book, your own Scrapbook, or put them in a frame to commemorate your activities years from now!

Below-take a few minutes and tell your ACTIVITY STORY. In your own words. Think of it as telling the story to your Grandchildren some day! Do it in your own words and handwriting-like your sending a post card to someone 50-100 years from now!

Our Family Wild Activity Story

_____

_____

_____

_____

_____

_____

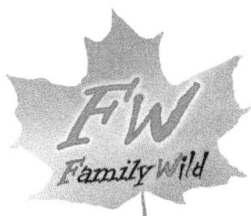
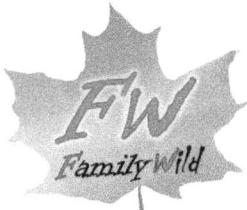

Bird Feeding Station

Objective: Create a home-made wild bird feeding station out of found and recycled materials

What You Might Need:

Wood - old pallets, used 2x4 lumber, two 8-foot wooden fence posts

or

Small old swing-set frame

Collection of cups and saucers of various sizes and colors from garage sales or resale stores

Wire or heavy twine

Concrete

Gorilla glue

Nails

Hammer, screw driver or drill

Bird seed, dried corn on the cob, oranges

Waxed cardboard or plastic milk or juice containers
Paint or stain or spar varnish

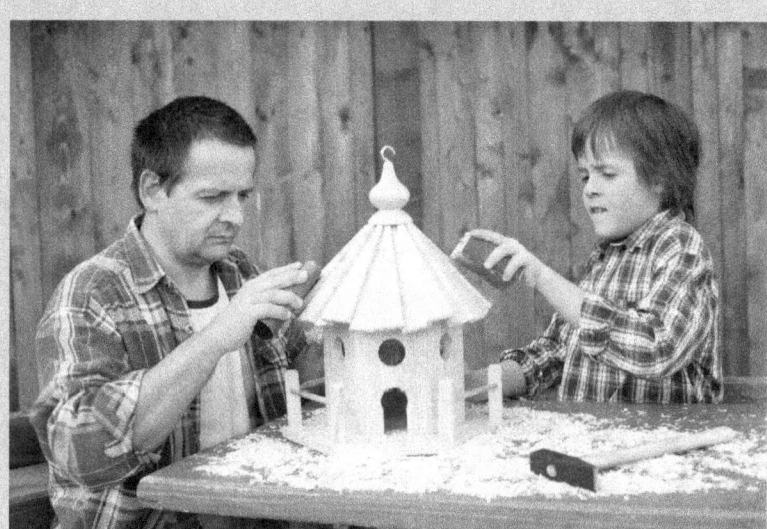

Jump in!

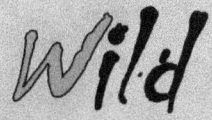

"Humans who spend time in the wilderness, alone, without man-made mechanical noise around them, often discover that their brain begins to recover its ability to discern things."

Robert Anderson

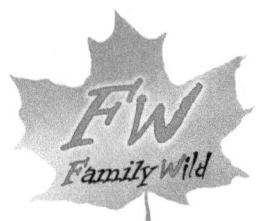

Note to adult helpers: This project may take more than one day - be willing to split each section up into an individual experience, especially if you are working with younger children.

Scope out your yard. Do birds come naturally? What kinds? Where do you see them most often? By watching for a few days, you'll get a sense of where the birds are already the most comfortable.

Where in the house would a bird viewing station be most visible for the entire family? How will the station affect both the inside view and the outside layout of your home? Now, if necessary, come to a compromise. For example, I notice birds mostly in my backyard, near the trees. But I only have one very small window that faces the back.

So I chose to position my feeders where they were visible to both the birds and our family - toward the back of the house but still in clear sight of my kitchen and study windows. Be patient - sometimes it takes a while for the birds to realize the bounty you have set out!

Creating the station

We'll be making some sort of frame to hold your birdfeeders. You can be quite creative here - maybe you can find an old swing set on Craig's List or at a garage sale or resale shop. If that is the case, just remove the swings and Keep the hooks and other hardware that will allow you to hang feeders and suet.

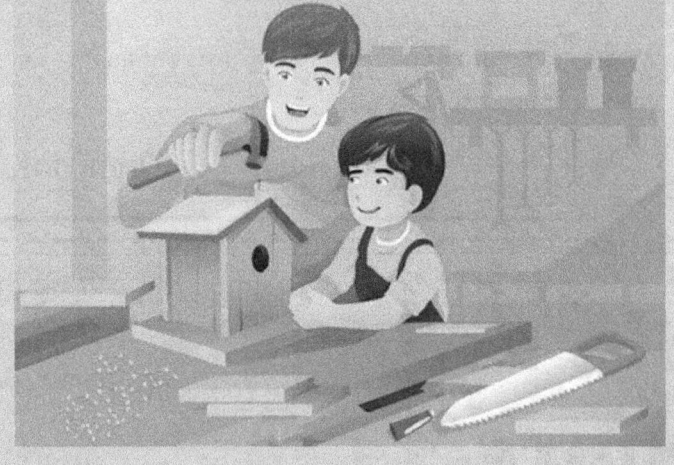

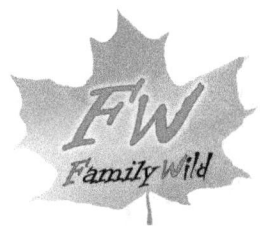

My parents very effectively use a couple of "repurposed" options - one is the metal clothesline in their backyard, the other, a simple post to which Dad attached curved shepherd hooks to support both flower baskets and hummingbird feeders.

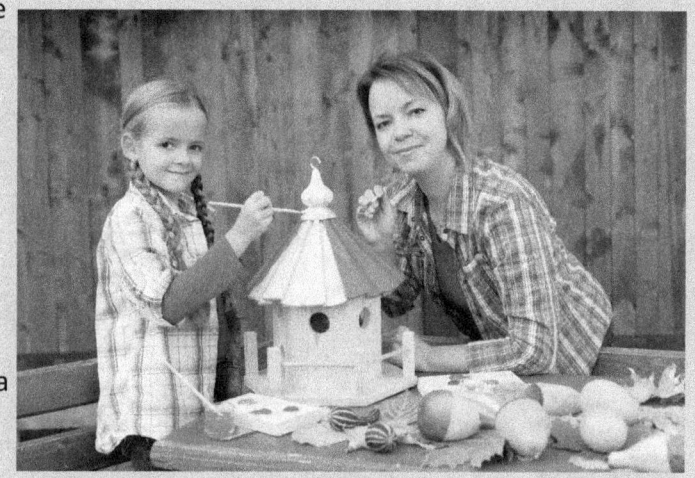

Otherwise, measure any repurposed wood that is sturdy enough to serve as a cross-bar to hang feeders from. Sink two wooden fence posts into your chosen bird-watching space, filling the holes with quick-set concrete if you wish to stabilize the support poles.

If you want to use hooks on the cross-bar, it's more comfortable to place them before attaching the cross bar to the support posts. I like hooks because I can easily remove and clean my feeders. Be sure to paint or treat the wood to give it a longer life.

Or, if you have limited space, try making a simple square with the boards from an old pallet. Lay three 1 foot sections side by side, then lay another two boards so they cut across the three you have placed in front of you.

Nail or screw through these boards to create the square. Nail or screw a rim around this square (to keep the bird seed from falling off or being easily scattered.)

If you are using a pallet board, you can affix this half-way above and half-way below the surface of your square. If you get too much of a lip, you won't be able to see the smaller birds.

Then mount this square on a single wood post or even attach it to a post on your deck. Be sure to paint or stain this feeder to help it last longer.

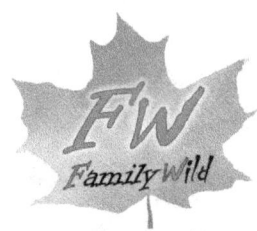

Make a "found object" bird bath and feeder:

Collect a nice bunch of old coffee cups and dinner plates, dessert plates, heavy vases, etc.

Lay all your treasures out on the floor or an outside work surface. Starting with the most stable plate, turn it over and glue a vase or heavy coffee mug to the bottom. Run a rim of glue around the vase or mug and this time, place a plate face up. Continue stacking like this until your bird bath or feeder is the height you want.

I often will top a "tower" like this with a very light serving dish or tray. Try to keep the heaviest items at the bottom and work up. Allow the creation to dry for a day, then move it outside near your bird feeding station.

This artistic feeder/birdbath also works well on porches or in back yards with very little extra space. Some plates can be filled with seed, other plates in the stack can be filled with water.

Use an old brush from a resale shop to sweep off used seed, leaves and dirt occasionally.

Cool things to hang from your station:

Waxed cardboard or quart milk-jug feeder- just cut two small squares out of the carton, leaving enough room at the bottom to puncture a hole for a heavy twig or piece of doweling to pass through the container. This is the perch for your dinner guests!

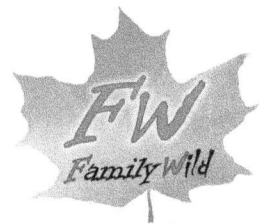

Run a string or piece of heavy wire through the top of the container, poor birdfeed in from the top (keep the cap!) and hang outside on your station.

Cut up an orange into four big pieces. "Sew" a piece of heavy yarn through the slice and make a loop. Hang the orange on your feeder. Drive long nails through a piece of pallet wood at an angle. Either nail this to your bird station or affix a loop to the top and hang it from the cross bar. You can push either dried corn cobs or orange slices onto the nails. If your family wants to invite squirrels in, this a good way to do it!

Go on to the next activity in this book-making a pine cone bird feeder!

There are endless ways to repurpose and reuse items. If you come up with a really neat birdfeeder, be sure to take a picture and upload it to the Family Wild website to share with others. Birdwatching is a life-long activity, and it always keeps you connected to the Wild.

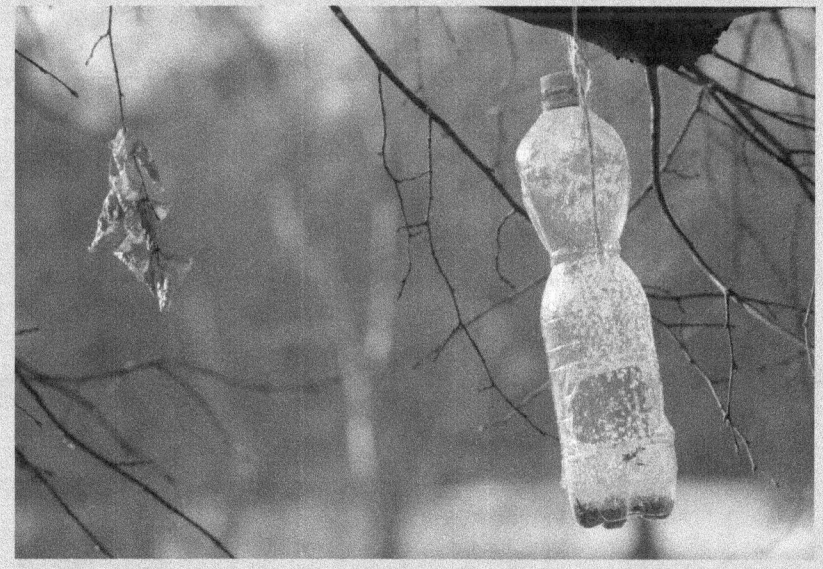

SCRAPBOOK PICTURES

Glue a couple pictures here
to remember your Activity

You can keep the pictures in Your Family Wild Activity book, your own Scrapbook, or put them in a frame to commemorate your activities years from now!

Below-take a few minutes and tell your ACTIVITY STORY.
In your own words. Think of it as telling the story to your Grandchildren some day! Do it in your own words and handwriting-like your sending a post card to someone 50-100 years from now!

Our Family Wild Activity Story

_____

_____

_____

_____

_____

_____

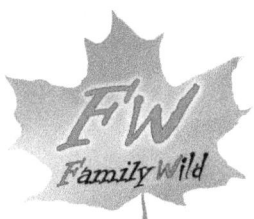 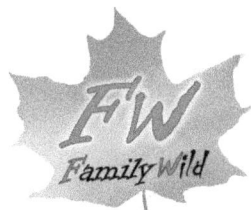

Simple Bird Treats

Objective: Create a simple birdfeed treat using natural objects and peanut butter

What You Might Need:

String

Scissors

Peanut butter

Bird seed

Small mixing bowl

Butter knife

Pinecones

An old towel drying rack or quilt display from Goodwill

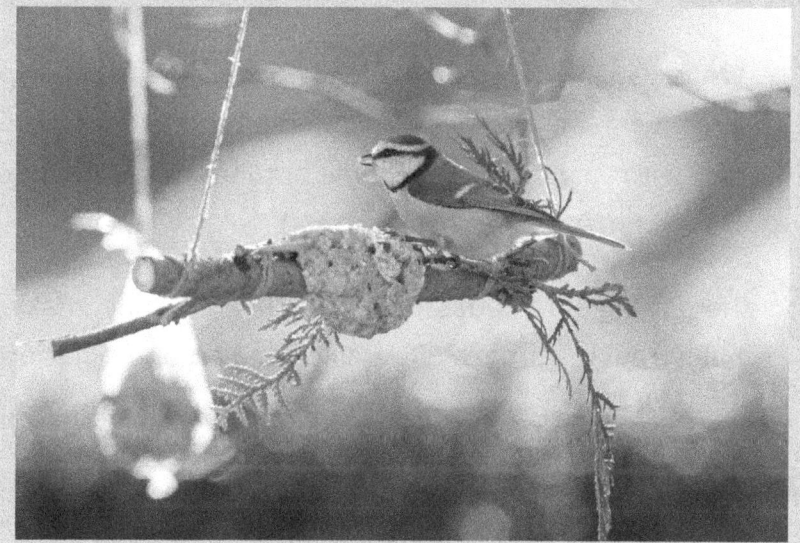

Jump in!

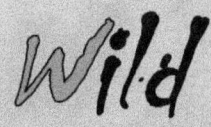

QUOTE

"What right do I have to be in the woods, if the woods are not in me?"

John Cage

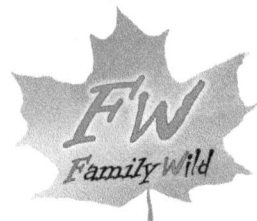

This activity is really easy and fun for even the youngest child. Take a nature walk and gather three or four heavy pinecones. You can also find these at art supply stores (especially during Christmas time) or even better, visit your local resale store.

While you are there, grab any towel drying or quilt display racks if you don't already have a place where you feed birds in your yard. (It's helpful to coat this rack with spare varnish or some outdoor metal treatment that will protect the wood or metal from the elements).

Tie a string around the top end of the pine cone, making a loop so it can be easily hung from the branch of a tree or tied around a stationary bird feedings station.

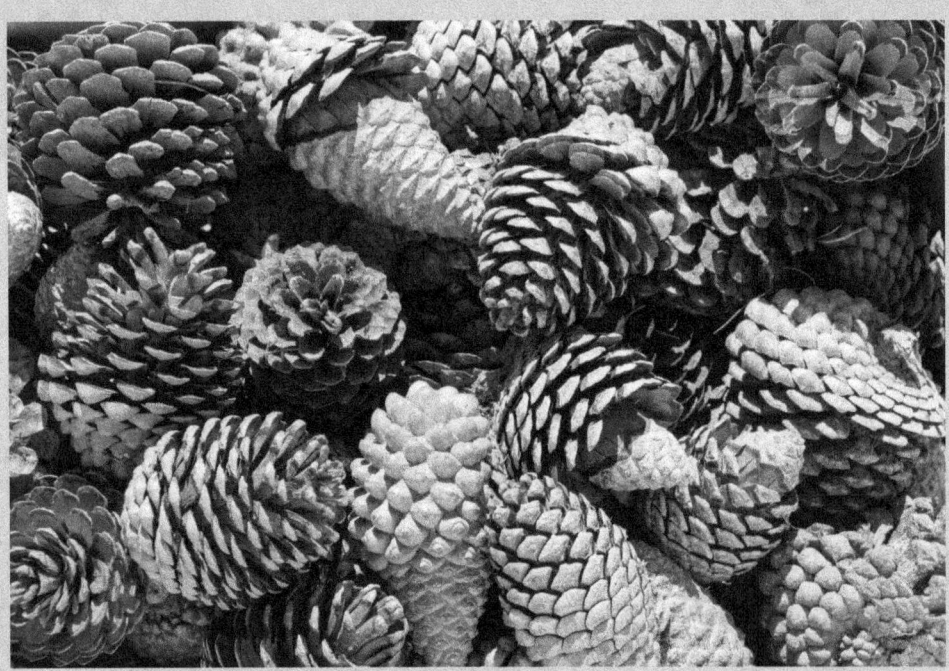

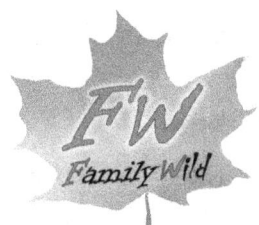

If you have the drying rack or quilt rack, the pinecones can hang from the horizontal parts.

Next, set out a pan to put your pinecones on. Mix together a cup of peanut butter and about ¼ cup of birdseed in a small bowl. Using a butter knife, smear the birdseed and peanut butter mixture on all the edges of the pinecone.

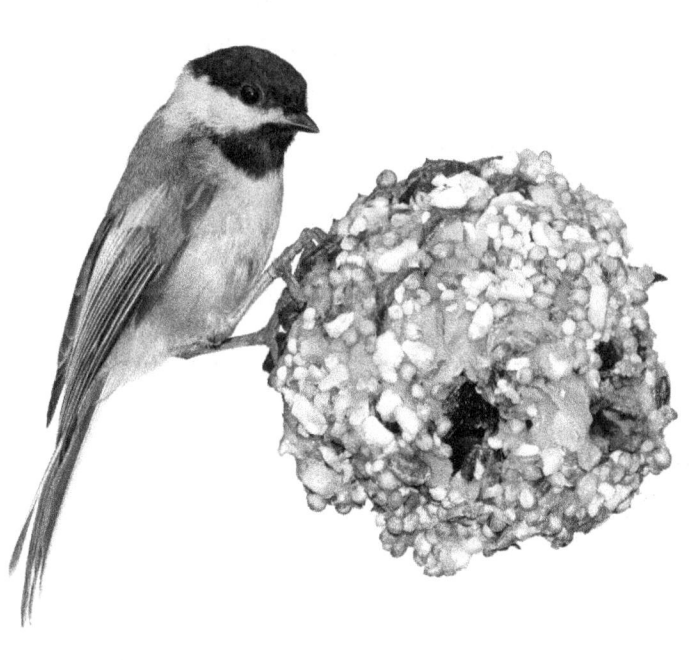

Take the pan outside and tie each pinecone to your bird feeding station. It's great fun to keep a list of what birds come to your new birdfeeder or even take pictures and start a file about what you see. Remember, if you get any great shots, submit them to Family Wild Online to share with others!

SCRAPBOOK PICTURES

*Glue a couple pictures here
to remember your Activity*

You can keep the pictures in Your Family Wild Activity book,
your own Scrapbook, or put them in a frame
to commemorate your activities years from now!

Below-take a few minutes and tell your ACTIVITY STORY.
In your own words. Think of it as telling the story to
your Grandchildren some day! Do it in your own words
and handwriting-like your sending a post card to
someone 50-100 years from now!

Our Family Wild Activity Story

_____

_____

_____

_____

_____

_____

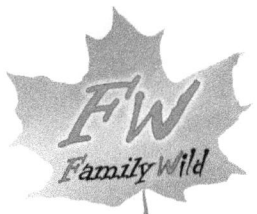 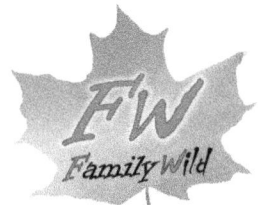

Recipes and Recipe Book

Objective: Compile a family recipe book, learning to keep track of measurements, cooking techniques and evaluate what worked...or didn't!

What You Might Need:

Small notebook that is easily stored in your kitchen or

Create a file on your word processor if you think you'll use it - it can be printed off and taken to a hunting camp or out on a family camping trip

Set of measuring spoons and measuring cups

Pans, skillets, slow-cooker

Jump in!

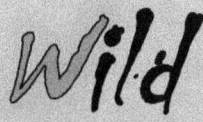

QUOTE

"If people concentrated on the really important things in life, there'd be a shortage of fishing poles."

Doug Larson

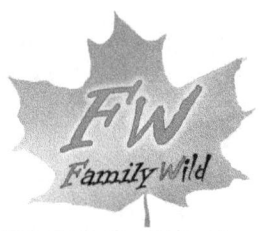

Preparing wild game, aside from basic fried fish, is a cooking skill that most folks find rather daunting. For instance, you don't usually see a packaged and frozen squirrel in the meat section at your local grocery store nor do you often find Ruffed Grouse recipes in Betty Crocker cook books.

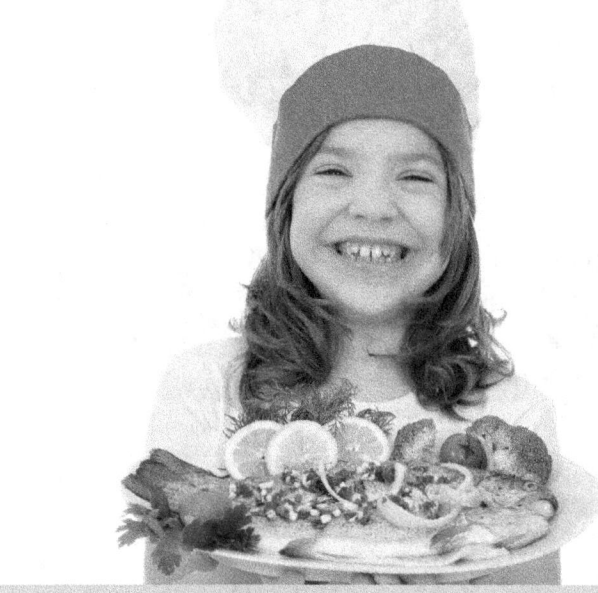

But I will be the first to tell you, squirrel is WONDERFUL when you know how to cook it - and I totally failed with my first grouse.

Thankfully, with the help of the internet, you can find a lot of very interesting and tasty recipes to try. Use those to start to get a sense of the basics - here are some questions you can answer for yourself:

What temperatures and times work best with the kind of meat you are trying to prepare? For instance, it is very easy to overcook venison!

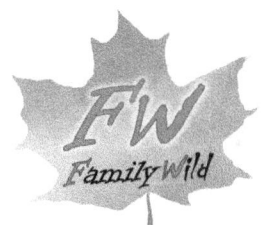

When does a slow-cooker work best? I love using a slow cooker with squirrel...I'll share an easy recipe at the end of this section.

What herbs and seasonings work best with this kind of fish?

With this cut of deer meat? With this wild turkey? Some herbs tend to mask some of the delicate fish fillets while others bring out the natural sweetness of the meat.

What vegetables or grains go great with this kind of fish or meat?

Once you've done a little research, pick one simple recipe to start with. Here is one:

BBQ Squirrel and Potatoes

One small onion

4-5 small potatoes, sliced in quarters

Beef broth

Italian seasonings

Your favorite BBQ sauce

Two or three dressed squirrels

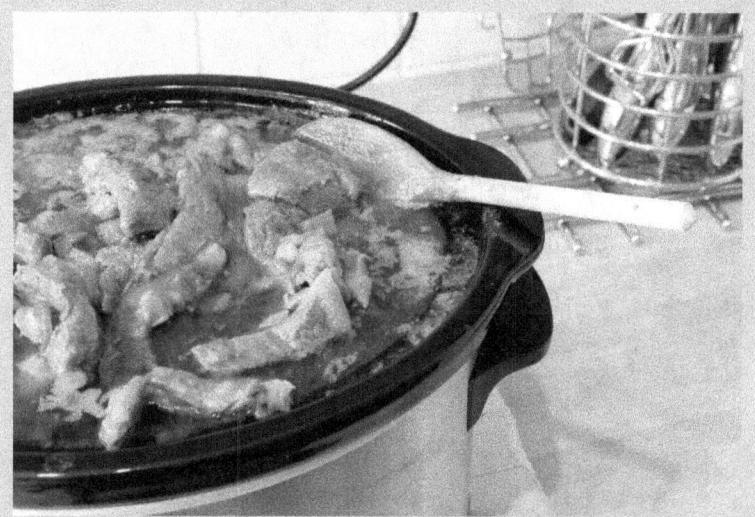

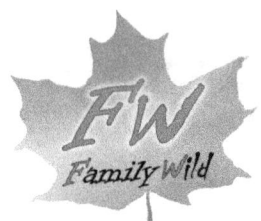

In a slow cooker, pour in about two cups of beef broth. Arrange the 3 squirrels in the bottom of the pan. (My slow-cooker is pretty big - I didn't have to cut up the squirrel into pieces but you may have to.) Cover squirrel with BBQ sauce and onions. Arrange potatoes along the sides of the meat. Sprinkle it all lightly with Italian seasonings.

Cover and slow-cook at 250 degrees F for four to five hours (squirrel sizes can vary a lot.) Meat should fall off the bones and the potatoes should be soft. You may choose to spoon the drippings over your potatoes - yum! Eat carefully, like you would a fish - squirrel has very small bones, too.

In your recipe book, jot down this technique and note any changes you made OR would make next time. Give the recipe a rating like five stars for something you want to do again soon or one star for "I don't like this one at all". Maybe you could prepare much the same recipe but use mushroom soup instead of BBQ sauce - be creative! That's always the first step in learning to live Wild.

SCRAPBOOK PICTURES

*Glue a couple pictures here
to remember your Activity*

You can keep the pictures in Your Family Wild Activity book,
your own Scrapbook, or put them in a frame
to commemorate your activities years from now!

Below-take a few minutes and tell your ACTIVITY STORY.
In your own words. Think of it as telling the story to
your Grandchildren some day! Do it in your own words
and handwriting-like your sending a post card to
someone 50-100 years from now!

Our Family Wild Activity Story

_____

_____

_____

_____

_____

_____

Family Wild

> "If you want to go fast, go alone. If you want to go far, go with others."
>
> African Proverb

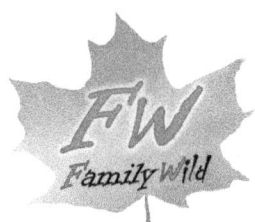
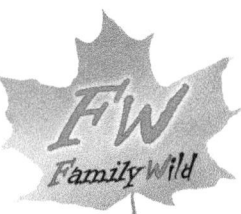

Dehydrator Fun!

Chapter 5: Dehydrator Fun

Objective: Learn how preserve harvested meats using a dehydrator

What You Might Need:

Mixing bowl
Sharp knife
Borrowed or purchased dehydrator unit
Lean cuts of meat
Dr. Pepper
Teriyaki Sauce
Air-tight containers

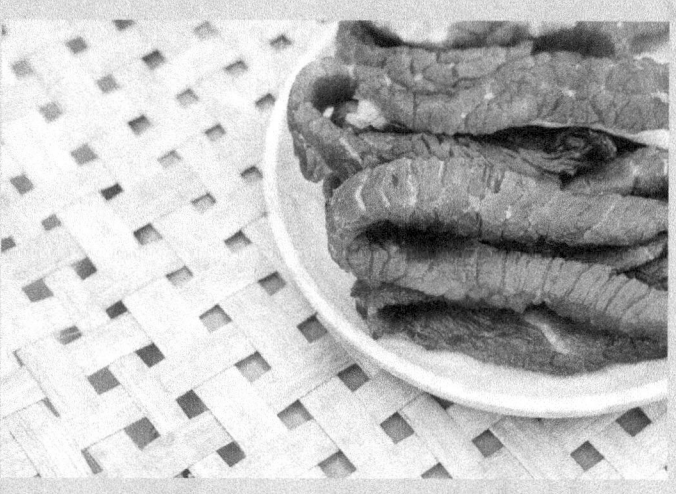

Jump in!

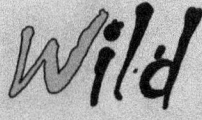

"As parents, grandparents, uncles and aunts we need to start getting out into nature with the young people in our lives. Families play a key role in getting kids outside."

David Suzuki

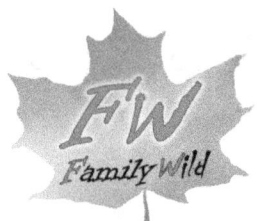

Dehydrators are a wonderful way to preserve some of your animal harvest.

Home-made jerky can make a lovely Christmas or birthday present for folks in your family, and it's a great way to take your meal with you on a hunting or fishing trip.

To begin, select a cut of meat that is lean and has no bones. If the meat is frozen, don't worry about thawing it out before you marinade it-partially frozen meat is actually easier to cut in thin strips. Slice the meat in about $1/8^{th}$ inch thick strips.

Place the strips in a mixing bowl and cover with Dr. Pepper and about ¼ cup of Teriyaki sauce. It's fun to add honey as well, for a sweeter jerky or sprinkle with chili powder for a little kick.

Allow the meat to marinate in the refrigerator over-night.

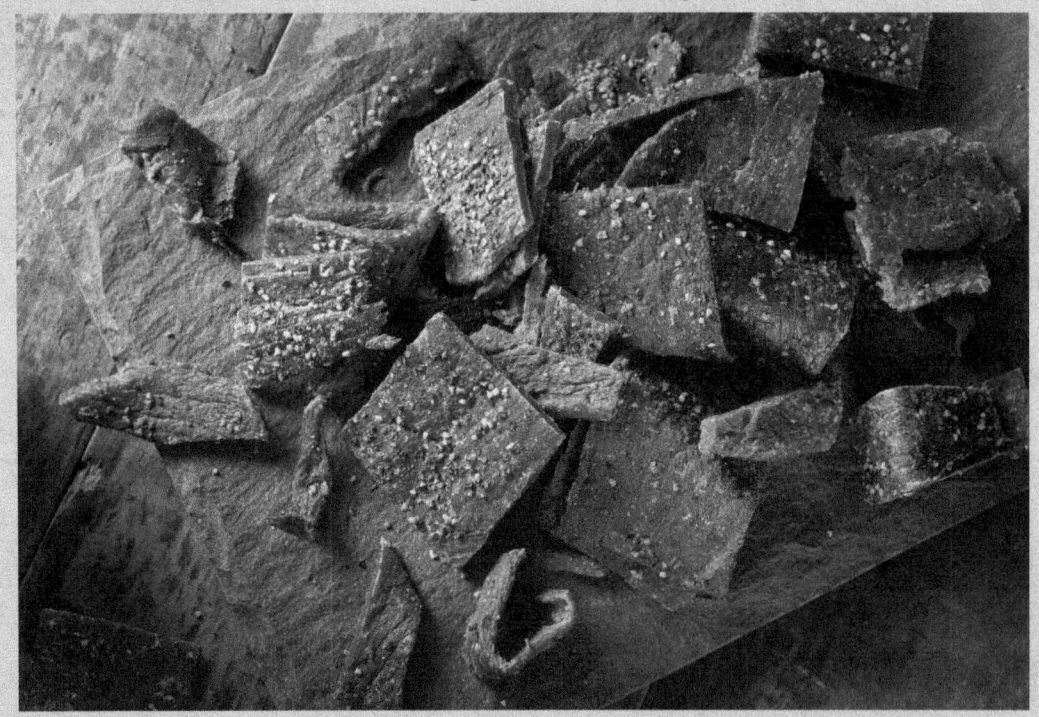

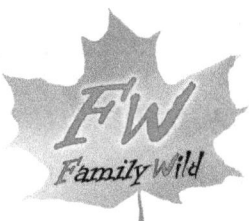

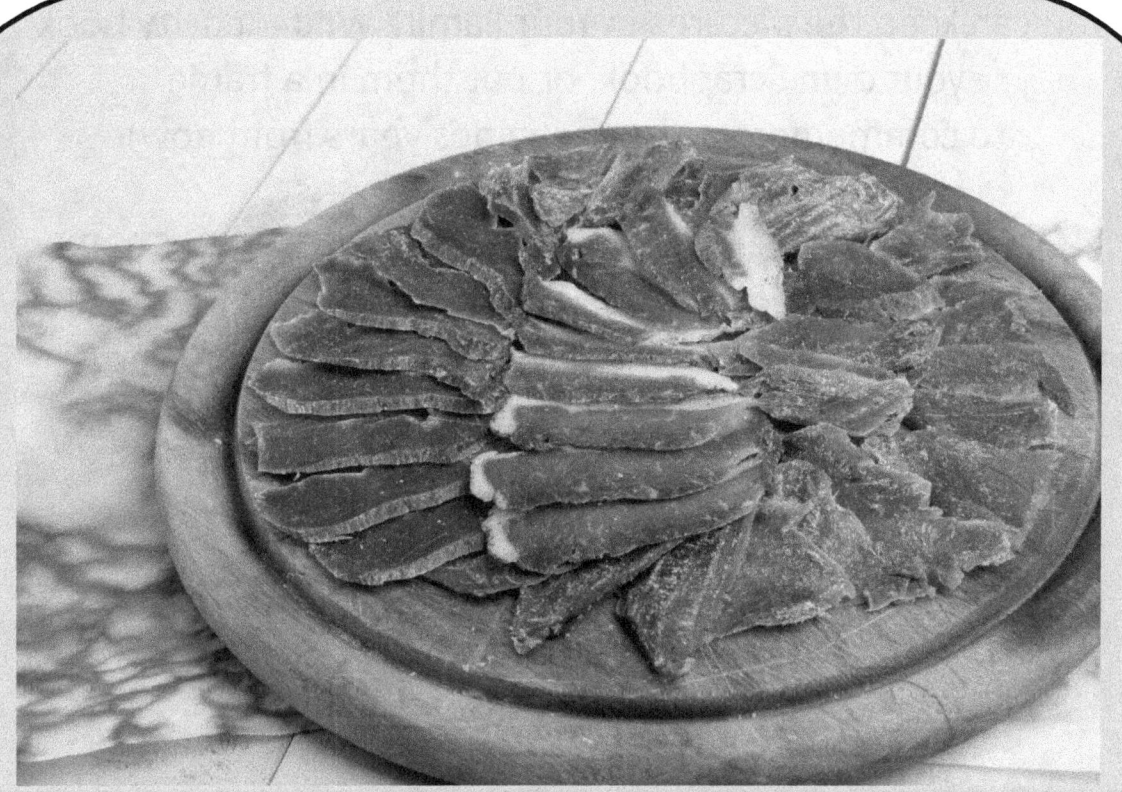

Adjust your dehydrator to meat settings--usually about 160 degrees F will do. You generally want to dehydrate the meat for about six hours.

The finished product will be slightly flexible and no red meat should show anywhere in the product. Some folks like to put the jerky into the over at 250 degrees for fifteen minutes to be sure all bacteria have been destroyed.

Store your jerky in an airtight container and keep out of the sunlight for longer shelf life. If you have a vacuum sealer, the jerky will last even longer.

Try different kinds of marinades-there are tons of good recipes on the internet for you to explore. Have fun Eating Wild!

SCRAPBOOK PICTURES

*Glue a couple pictures here
to remember your Activity*

You can keep the pictures in Your Family Wild Activity book, your own Scrapbook, or put them in a frame to commemorate your activities years from now!

Below-take a few minutes and tell your ACTIVITY STORY.
In your own words. Think of it as telling the story to your Grandchildren some day! Do it in your own words and handwriting-like your sending a post card to someone 50-100 years from now!

Our Family Wild Activity Story

_____

_____

_____

_____

_____

_____

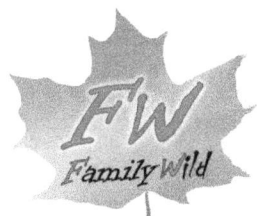
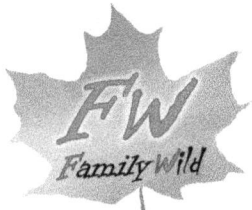

Pressing Flowers

Objective: Learn to preserve fresh flowers, identify flower species, and keep a flower journal.

What You Might Need:

Six 12" x 12" pieces of plywood
Drill
Long screws with washers and nuts
Paper Towel
Three ring binder
Plastic sheet protectors
Sharpie fine-tip marker
Art materials of your choice to decorate your press with.

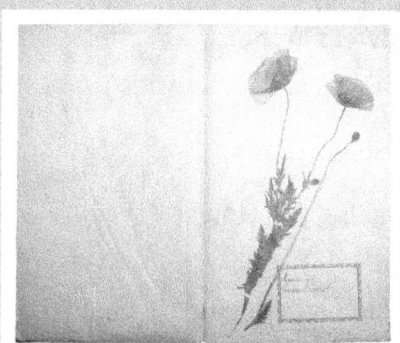

Flower identification book for your state or internet access via smartphone or computer

Small spiral notebook and pen

Camera or smart phone

Scissors

Jump in!

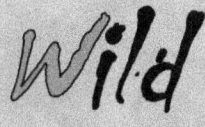

QUOTE

"Kids are naturally gifted at art from a very young age. The problem is when they get older and become self-conscious. The process should always be fun, though."

Damien Hirst

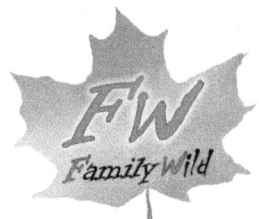

This is a sweet little activity for children of all ages, once an adult has helped with putting the flower press together. It encourages families to learn more about the flowers in their yards, fields and woods, and to identify species that are protected (and why) as well as species that can be harvested and used to make lovely dried flower art.

Making the Flower Press:

First, scrounge up six pieces of 12"x12" plywood. Try to select pieces without any warp in them. Thinner boards do work fine.

Drill four holes, one in each corner. The holes should line up - they will be threaded with screws to create the even pressure of the press.

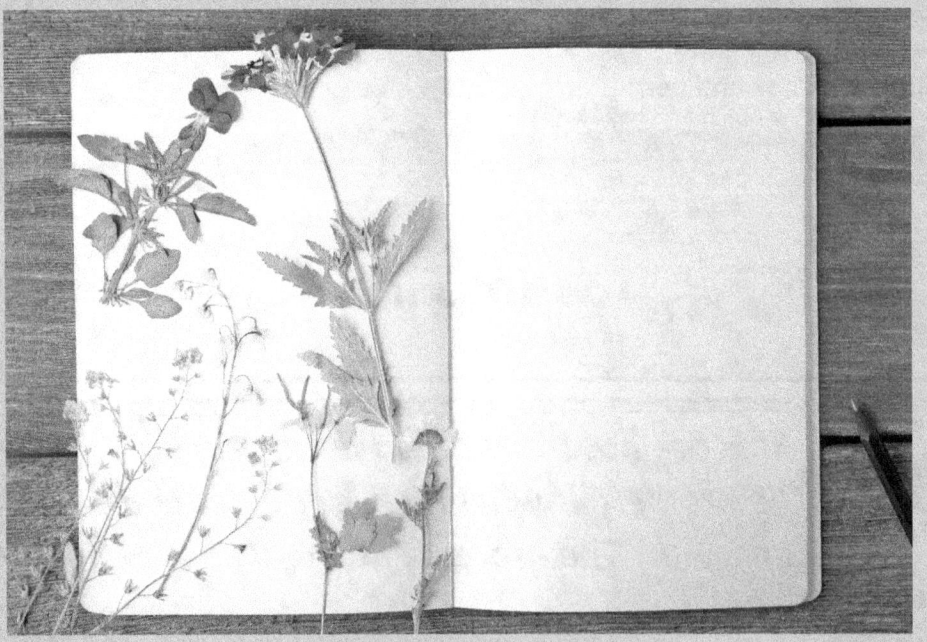

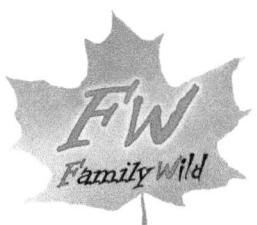

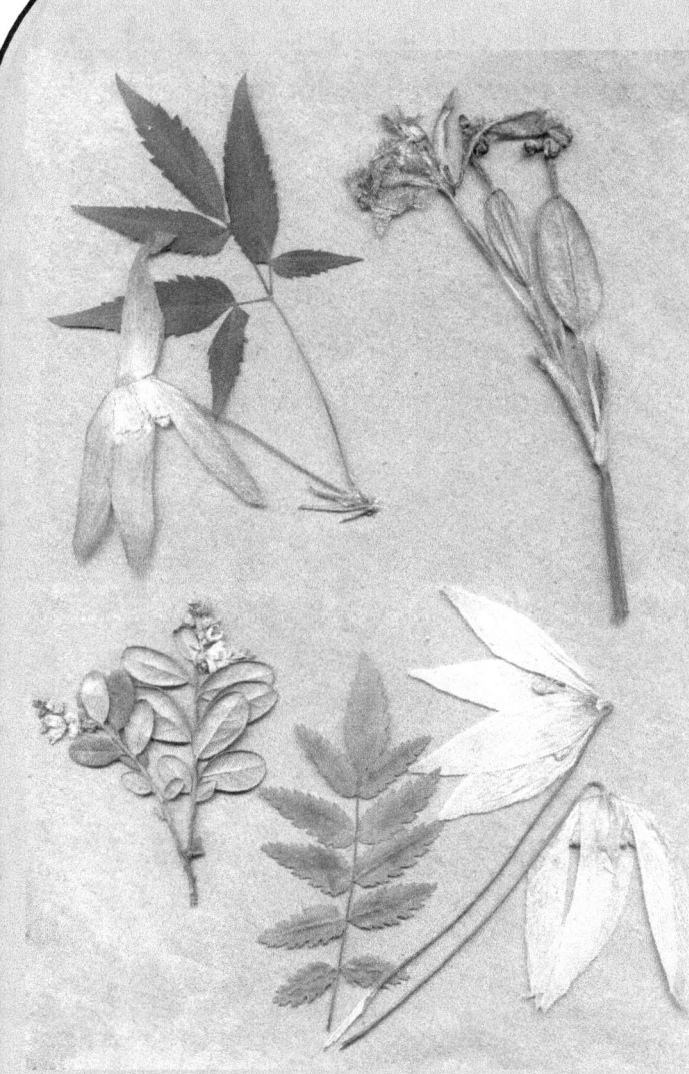

Paint the top and bottom boards and decorate however you wish- sharpies work great on wood and last a long time. Add your name and date to the project or put on a Family Wild sticker. Make it yours!

Collecting and pressing flowers

First, go flower hunting and take your press with you. This is a great activity in the warmer spring and summer and early fall months.

Identify the flower before you pick it. In some cases, flowers may be protected. If you not allowed to harvest this variety, make a note in your small spiral notebook -what kind of flower was it?

How many were in the area? Was there anything neat or unusually about this flower? Take a picture of it with a camera or cell phone! Remember to set your device to do close-up shots and try not to get your shadow in the way!

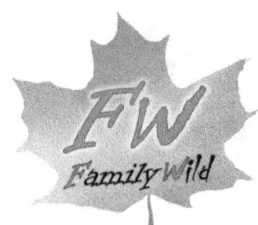

If you are allowed to harvest this flower, carefully cut the flower and a small length of stem. If there are quite a few of this flower around, cut three or four to press.

Open up your press. Place one sheet of absorbent paper down on the bottom of your press, and arrange your flowers on the paper. Cover with another sheet of absorbent paper and one board of your press. Screw the layers together firmly. In your note book, list the kind of flower you harvested, when in the day you cut the flower and where you found it. Be sure to date it as well.

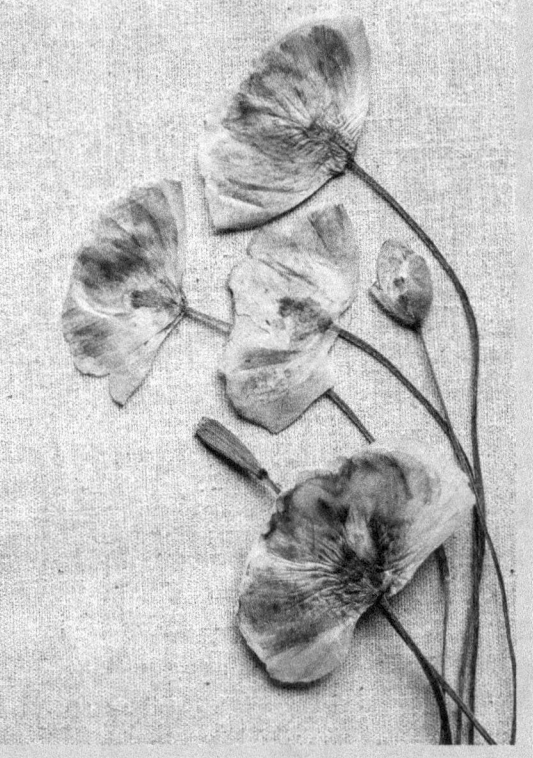

As you continue to hunt, follow the instructions above - identify, cut, put flower between two sheets of paper, place the next board, tightly screw the press together, make a note of what you found, where, when and any special notes about the flower you want to add.

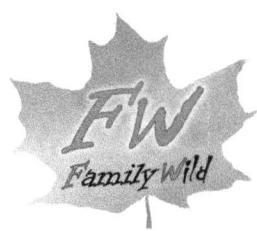

It's fun to also take pictures of what you harvested - include your family members in your pictures! You can add these pictures to your flower journal.

Now the waiting. It's best to keep the press tightly screwed together and in a cool and dry part of your home for at least a week.

Prepare your Journal:

Be sure you have a few plastic protector sheets (that you can slide paper in so that it is protected on both sides) and a 3 ring binder at hand.

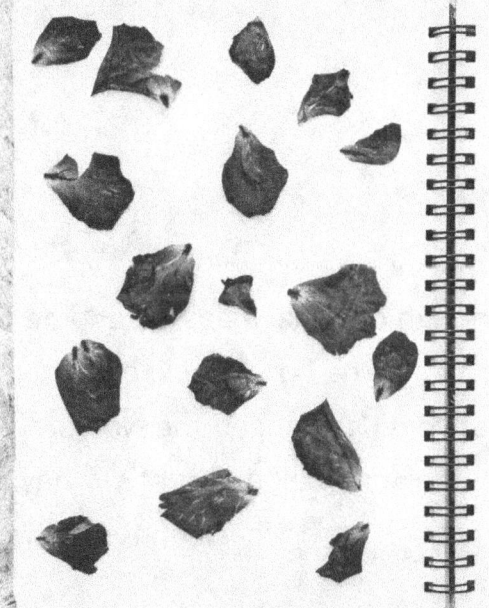

Decorate or label the outside and spine of your binder anyway you wish.

Add picture and information about the flowers you could not pick but found in the woods or fields or along the beach. Try drawing a few on your own!

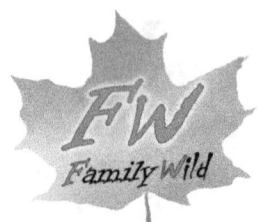

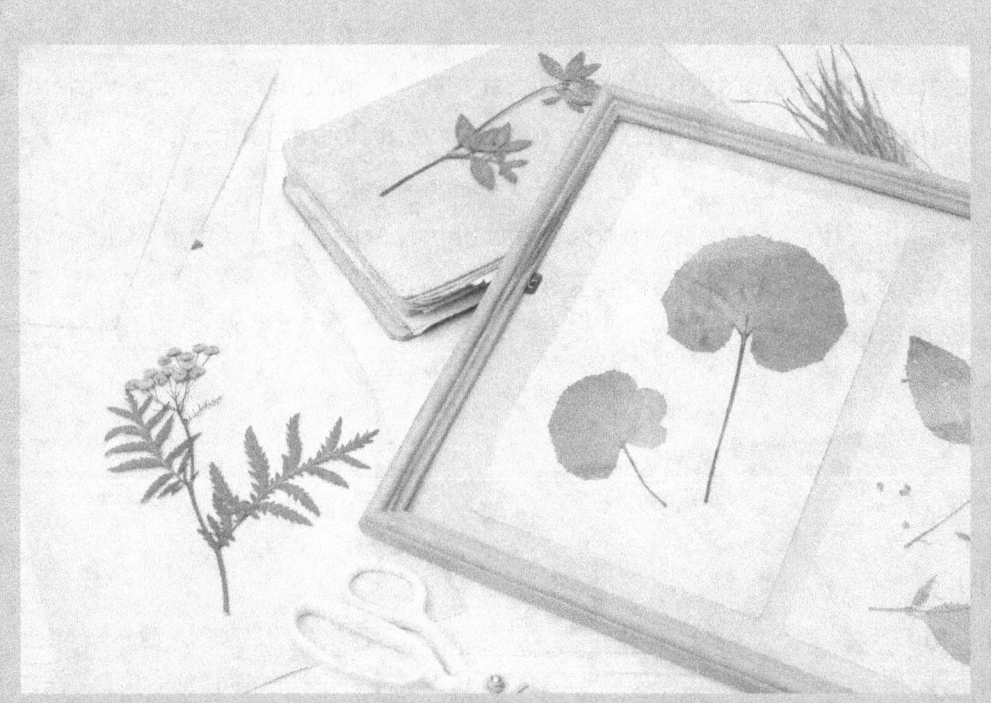

Gently open the press after enough days have passed and be very, very careful as you peel the absorbent paper away. The flowers will be very delicate. Take the time to notice how drying and pressing changed the way they look…did the colors change? Do the petals or stem look or smell different? If they aren't totally dry yet, replace the paper and tighten the press back up for a few more days.

If the flowers are dry, transfer them to a piece of heavy dark paper or cardstock - choose a color that best shows off their petals. Use just a tiny drop of glue to hold the flower in place on the paper. Once it has dried, add a label to the paper with the name of the flower and the date and any other information you want to add.

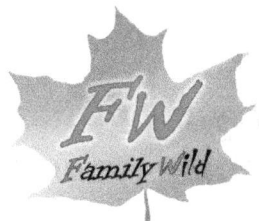

Slide the sheet with its attached flowers very carefully into a plastic cover sheet and place in your three ring binder.

Dried flowers can be a great deal of fun. You can paste many kinds onto note cards to create your own special stationery to send to family and friends, make wall hangings using old picture frames and their glass inserts, decorate the outside of journals, on and on.

Check out our blog—occasionally you'll find other neat things to do with your Wild flower press!

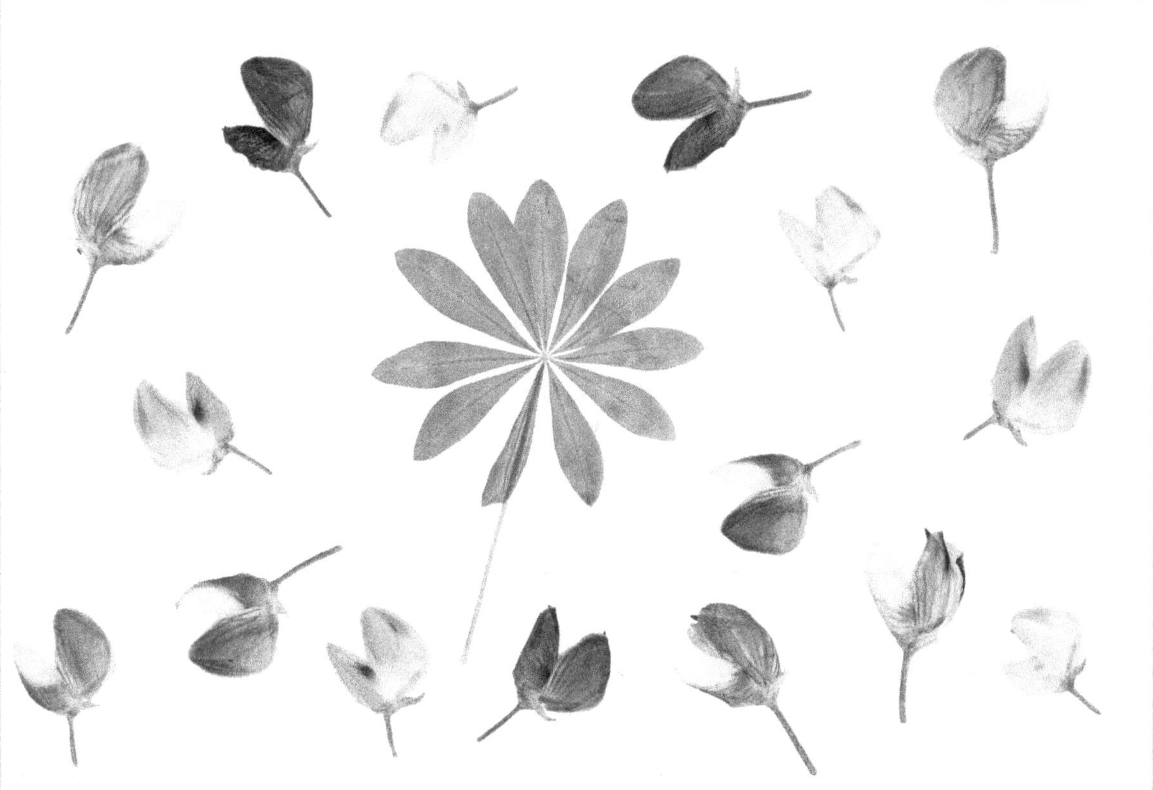

SCRAPBOOK PICTURES

Glue a couple pictures here
to remember your Activity

You can keep the pictures in Your Family Wild Activity book, your own Scrapbook, or put them in a frame to commemorate your activities years from now!

Below-take a few minutes and tell your ACTIVITY STORY. In your own words. Think of it as telling the story to your Grandchildren some day! Do it in your own words and handwriting-like your sending a post card to someone 50-100 years from now!

Our Family Wild Activity Story

_____

_____

_____

_____

_____

_____

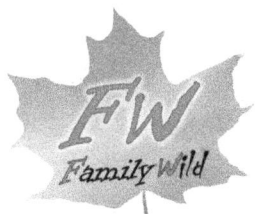
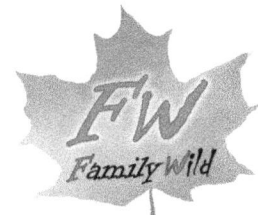

Hunting/Fishing Journal

Objective: Use simple materials to create a journal record of nature-based activities, including art, writing, photographs, weather conditions, water condition and other interesting data.

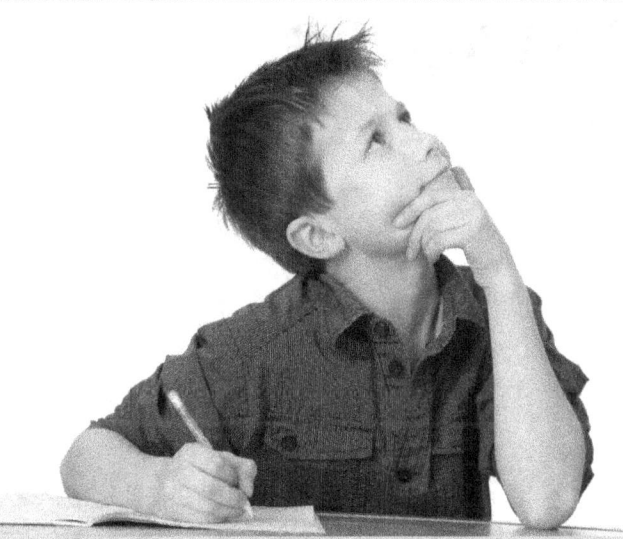

What you may need:

Loose leaf paper -plain and lined

Hole punch

An inexpensive 2 inch three-ring binder

Art supplies to taste- colored pencils or non-bleed pens, pencils, paper glue, scrapbooking scissors, etc.

Camera (on your cell phone is fine if you can download and print images)

Jump In!

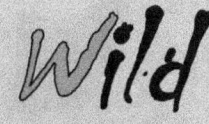

QUOTE

"Everyone likes birds. What wild creature is more accessible to our eyes and ears, as close to us and everyone in the world, as universal as a bird?"

David Attenborough

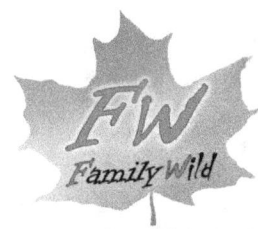

You experience so much in nature! Sometimes, you don't really understand how much information you're taking in, how much you are being challenged and changed by your activities in the natural world.

A journal becomes a handy way to store information, play with new ideas, express and capture the profound and the funny – not to mention passing on your memories to future generations!

So find yourself an inexpensive 2 inch 3 ring-binder. You can buy one new or keep an eye out at garage sales or resale shops like Goodwill. Keep a stock of paper for yourself, both the lined kind and plain copy paper.

If you want more color or texture you can use any kind of paper in your journal - the special papers that scrap-bookers use can add color and interest to your work. Now you are ready to start!

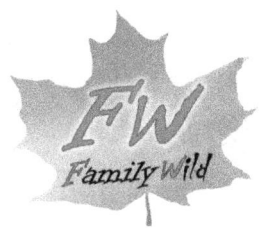

Create a nice cover your journal, either with your own art or with photographs you have taken. Be sure to put a start date on the cover and on the spine of your journal; when you get to be fifty or sixty years old, you may have a small collection of journals and it's helpful to be able to quickly find what you are looking for.

So what do you put in it? Here are a few ideas:

Weather conditions for the day you went hunting or fishing

Water or land conditions on the day of your hunting or fishing trip

Anything special you noticed in the water or in the woods - an unusual bird, strange lichen, the smell of the autumn leaves, the skunk in your blind!

Your pictures, poetry, or artwork

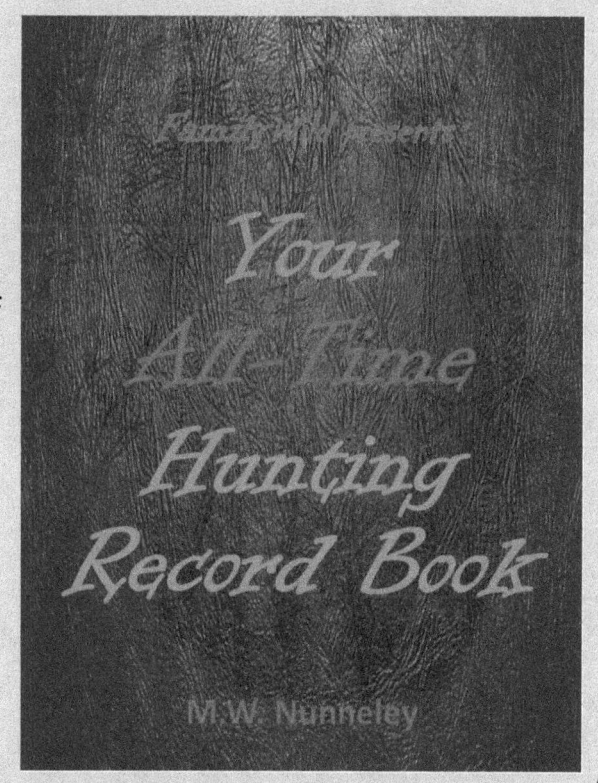

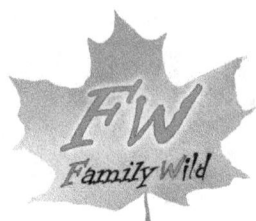

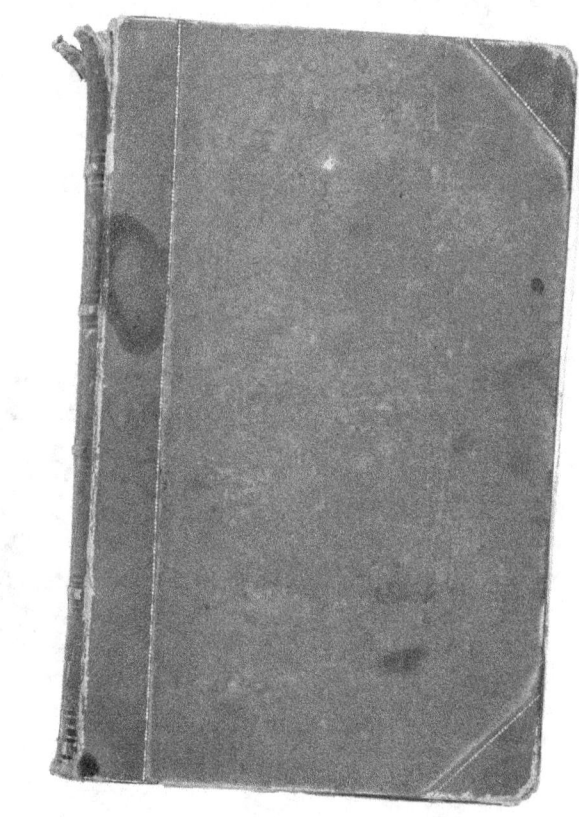

What you caught or shot on what day - be sure to add when, where, how you bagged your catch, field dressing or cleaning thoughts and how it all made you FEEL! And pictures are, as they say, "worth a thousand words".

Descriptions and pictures of any construction projects you've done - a deer blind, a small game garden, a worm composter. What worked well? What would you do differently next time? Did anything frustrate or surprise you?

The list is really endless - the journal, unlike a diary, is meant to be sketched in, written sideways and upside down in, filled with comics and pictures and bits of really serious grouchy words when you feel like it.

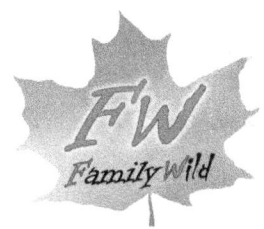

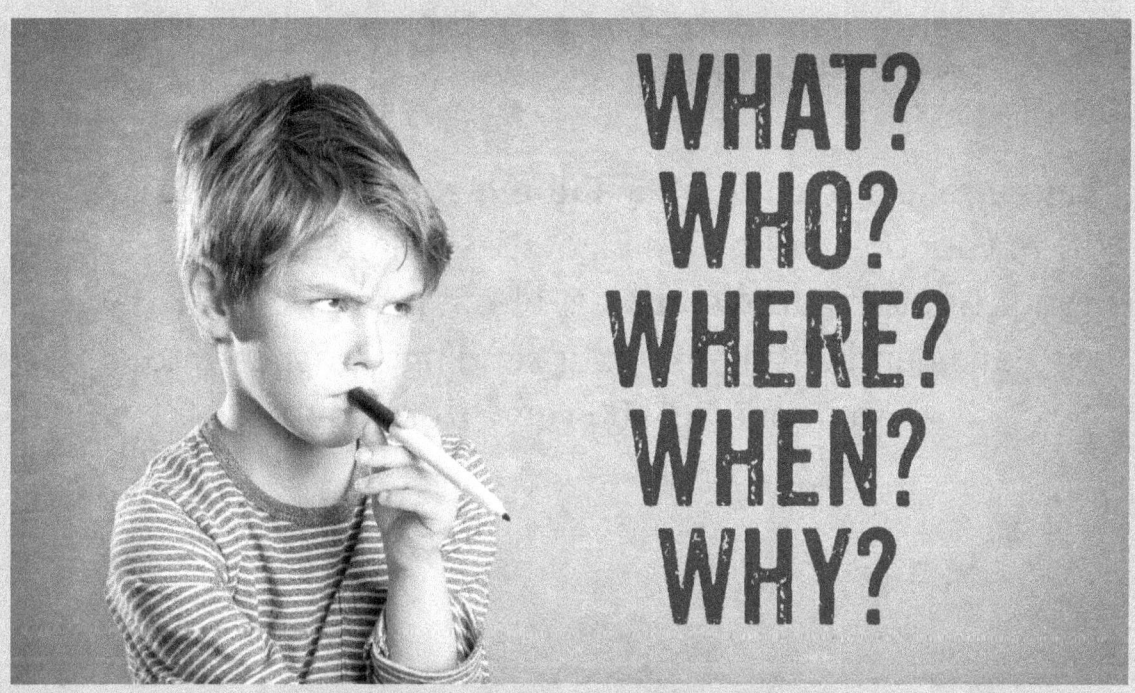

In other words, you make it your own and have FUN doing it when the weather is not cooperating enough for you to be out in the woods or on the lake. You might add to it every day or maybe only a couple of times a year. It's there for YOU and just for you.

But the magic? Someday this journal could be passed down to your grandchildren, great-grandchildren and beyond. It will become a treasure of who you "were" and what life was like years ago. It will show your Wild side!

SCRAPBOOK PICTURES

Glue a couple pictures here
to remember your Activity

You can keep the pictures in Your Family Wild Activity book, your own Scrapbook, or put them in a frame to commemorate your activities years from now!

Below-take a few minutes and tell your ACTIVITY STORY. In your own words. Think of it as telling the story to your Grandchildren some day! Do it in your own words and handwriting-like your sending a post card to someone 50-100 years from now!

Our Family Wild Activity Story

_____

_____

_____

_____

_____

_____

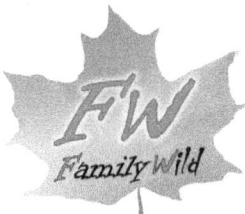
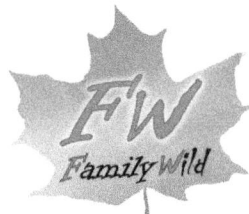

Poetry and Nature

Objective: To use words to express, in simple poetic form, experiences in nature.

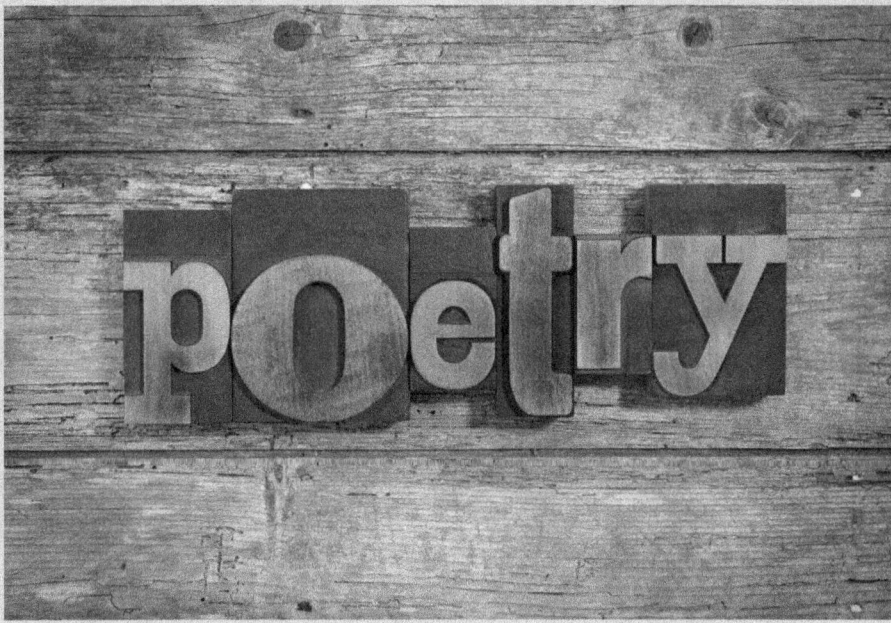

What You May Need:

A lined writing binder, small journal or computer-where do you like to write?

Pen/pencil if working on paper

Small pocket-sized notebook

Jump In!

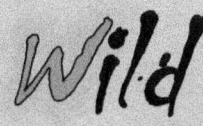

QUOTE

"In nature there are few sharp lines."

A. R. Ammons

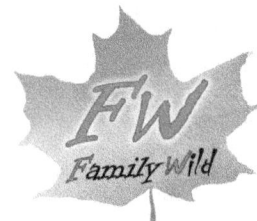

I know - poetry is a scary word for most folks. But it doesn't have to be. Here, try this first experiment!

Write the words "I am" on your paper.

Look outside and wait for your eye to fall on something, anything---a leaf, a cloud, the way the grass is moving in the wind, an upside down bird at the feeder, an apple falling off the tree, waves wiggling up onto the beach, a flower growing out of an old picnic table.

Add a word or phrase about what you see to "I am".

Write another "I am", this time noticing what you hear.

Add another " I am", this time jotting down what you smell.

Do another "I am" line, capturing what you can taste.

Doodle another "I am" line, describing what you can touch.

Create one more "I am" line, noticing what you feel or think.

So your "poem" could look something like this-

I am ice bending the pine,

I am the chickadee fussing at the woodpecker

I am the awakening spring-perfumed mud

I am the sugar in a Maple's blood,

I am the suet bumpy with seeds

I am me, wondering Easter thoughts.

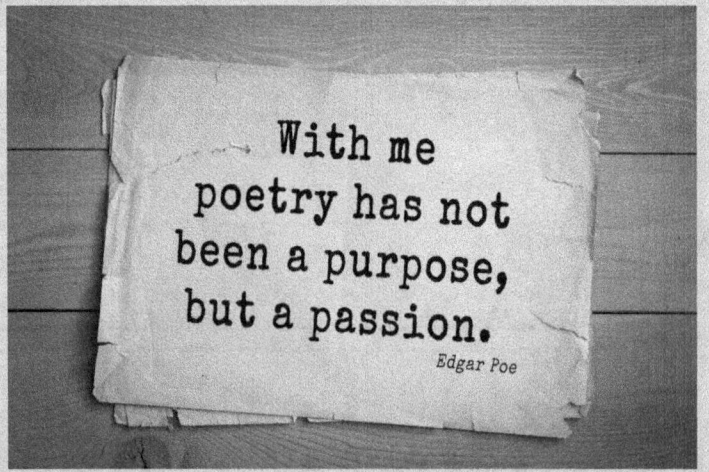

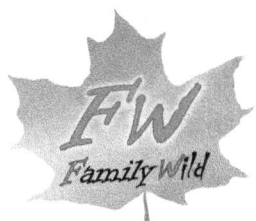

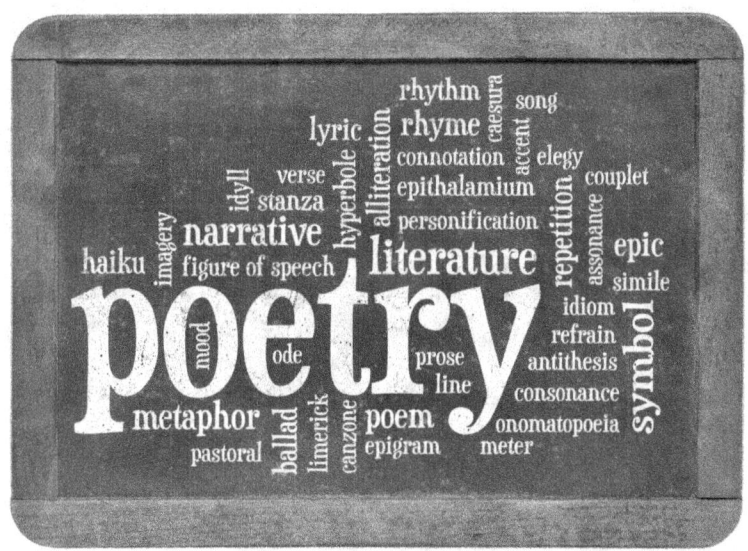

Yup! It's just that easy to write this kind of poem. It's great fun for your friends and family to each scribble the six lines and then read them out-loud, one right after the other, to create an even longer and richer work.

Here is another fun way to write a poem:

Gather four photographs you have taken in nature or go on the internet or in a book and pick four. They can really be of anything and if they are not all the same, your poem will be even better!

Lay the pictures out in an up and down row, like lines on a paper. Place a piece of paper next to the pictures. Begin with your first picture - write one word, or a short descriptive phrase. For example, if I have a picture of a tree I might write something like "ancient bare branches" or "twigs scratch the sky" or even just "old maple". Simple is beautiful!

Skip a line on your paper.
Write a word or phrase for your second picture.
Skip a line.

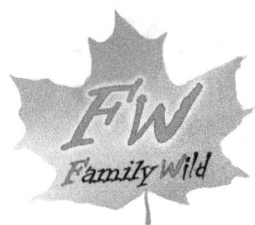

Write a word or phrase for your third picture.

Skip a line.

Write a word or phrase for your fourth picture.

Now, take the pictures away. You should have four lines of writing, with a space between each line.

On the empty line, write how you feel or bring in some action. So, if you wrote, "old maple", you might add something like "lonely in the pasture" or "waving its arms in joy".

Fill in the other blank lines with feeling or action lines.

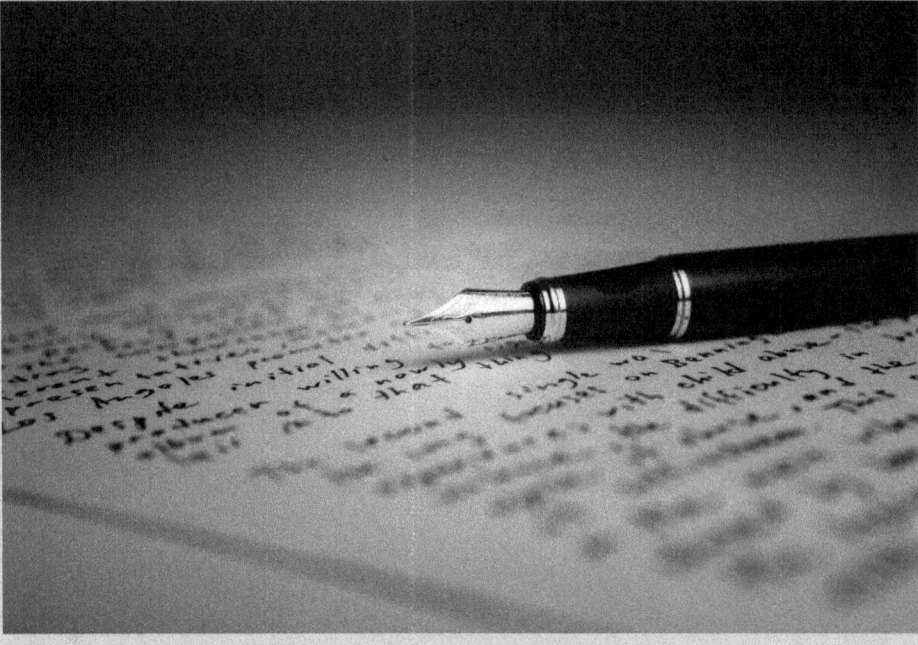

For the very last line, try to sum up what you think the poem is trying to say. So here is what I might do…notice the last line pulls all the rest together:

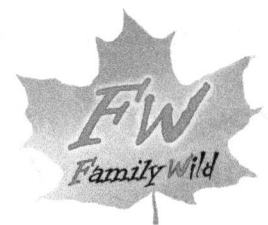

Old Maple
Waving her arms in joy
Chickadee all fluffed up
Springs away in alarm
The fallen cedar
Chuckles and snuggles the earth
My bent fishing pole
HUMS SUMMER TO IT ALL.

And that is all there is to it…four pictures, eight lines and you have a neat poem. Of course, there are many, many ways to write poems! Experiment with your own kinds, play with other forms. But never let the words scare you! After all, you are WILD!

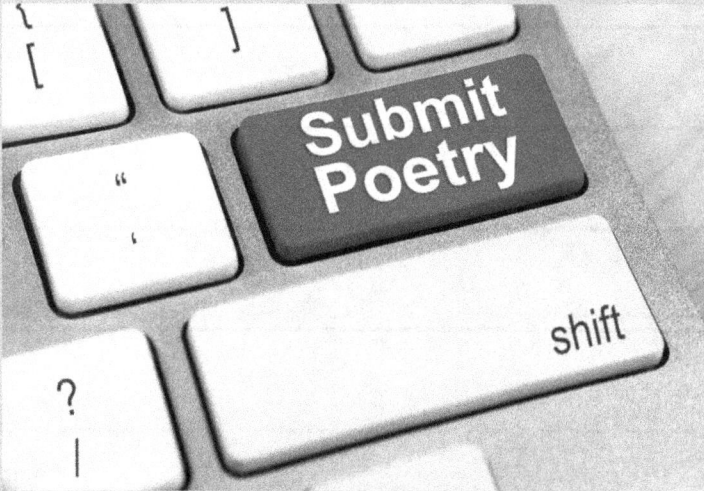

SCRAPBOOK PICTURES

Glue a couple pictures here
to remember your Activity

You can keep the pictures in Your Family Wild Activity book,
your own Scrapbook, or put them in a frame
to commemorate your activities years from now!

Below-take a few minutes and tell your ACTIVITY STORY.
In your own words. Think of it as telling the story to
your Grandchildren some day! Do it in your own words
and handwriting-like your sending a post card to
someone 50-100 years from now!

Our Family Wild Activity Story

_____

_____

_____

_____

_____

_____

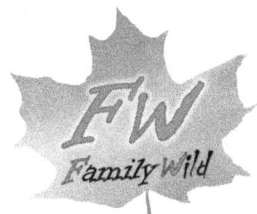 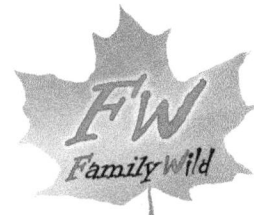

Wildlife Journalism

Objective: Write a simple article for a local newspaper sharing one Family Wild nature project.

What You Might Need:

Access to a Computer and printer

Internet access (usually available at your local library or college if you don't have home access)

Black and white pictures in Jpeg file format or glossy image that can be scanned by the paper

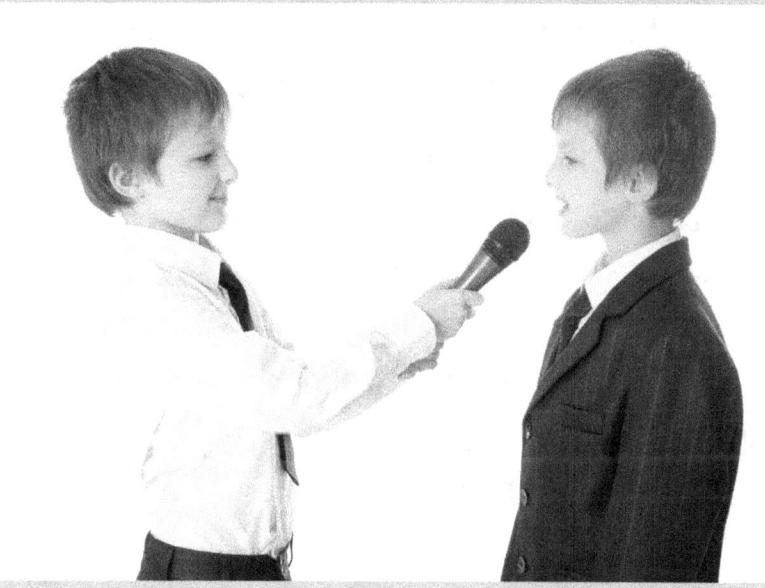

Jump in!

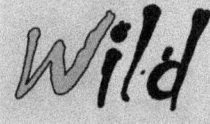 **QUOTE**

"Everyone likes birds. What wild creature is more accessible to our eyes and ears, as close to us and everyone in the world, as universal as a bird?"

David Attenborough

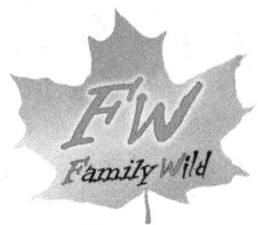

Through-out this book, you've been learning interesting things and doing fun projects. The time may come when you want to share what you are doing with folks in your home town. Very often, newspapers are looking for family interest stories to put in their paper. And writing for them isn't as scary or hard as it sounds. Here are a few pointers to get you started:

Identify your local paper and find out the name of the person who "edits" the part of the paper you are interested in writing for. For instance, if you are sharing your experience of taking pictures of wildlife, that might appear in the arts section.

If you want to voice your concern about trash you found in the woods, that might fall in an "editorial" section. Usually, if you call or email the newspaper, they'll help you find the right department and the right contact person.

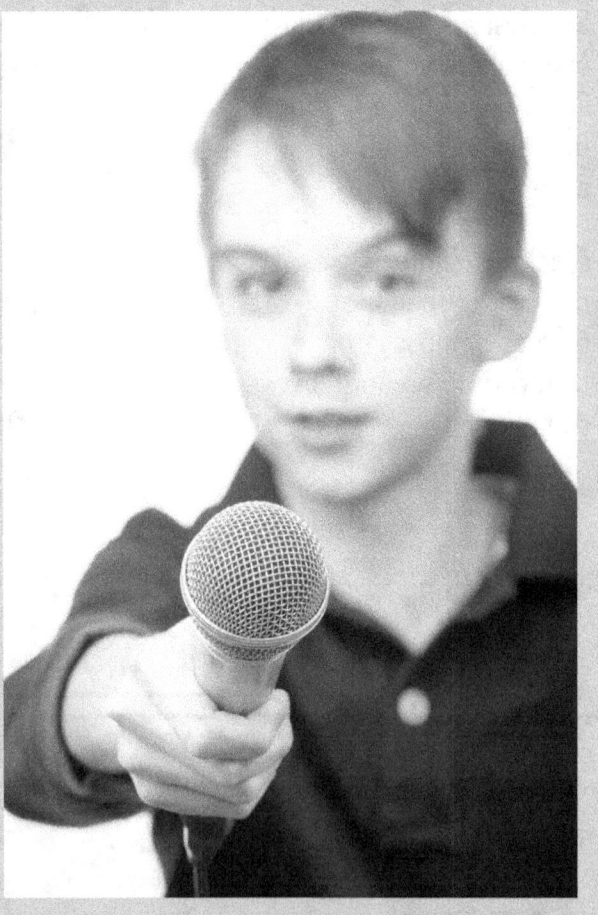

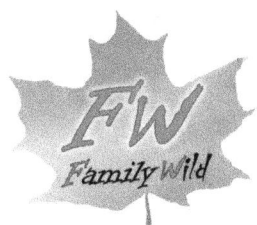

Once you know who to talk to at the newspaper, ask them how long your article should be and if they would like pictures to accompany the written words.

If so, be sure to ask how they would like the pictures delivered to them or in what electronic format. If you aren't sure how to do that, ask! Or look it up on You Tube! Or go to your local library and find someone to help you. The information is there - just be willing to find it!

Write your article. Usually, in a newspaper you would try to answer these easy questions - what did you do, when did you do it, where did you do it, why did you do it, who helped, and what did you learn or what happened when you did it.

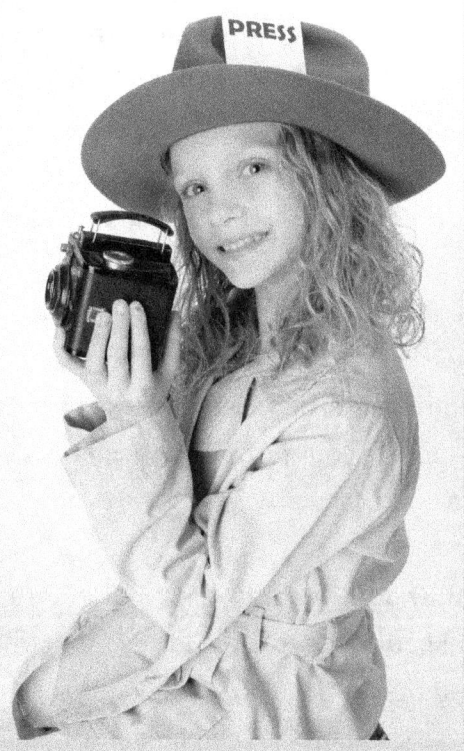

For instance, if you are sharing your first great coyote photograph, you'll want to explain what camera or cell or game camera you used, where you took the shot, why you liked taking pictures of the coyote and what you do with your wildlife pictures, who was there helping out, and what happened to the coyote when the flash went off.

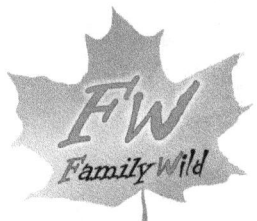

Let the article sit for a few days then share it with your family. Listen carefully to what they say...maybe some words are spelled wrong or maybe they are really amazed at your writing skills.

Maybe the article is too long, or you forgot the part when the coyote turned and swished his tail before you took that shot. Or share the article with your teacher, your grandparent, an older friend - anyone who can read it and help you make it even better.

Submit the article to the newspaper. Be sure to include your pictures and your NAME at the end of the article!

If they don't want to print it, don't fret or feel bad! Keep trying and keep a journal with the writing you've done for the paper - these short articles can be part of your own Nature Blog or Facebook Page, too! And even more important, this kind of writing is a picture of what you are learning and who you are right now.

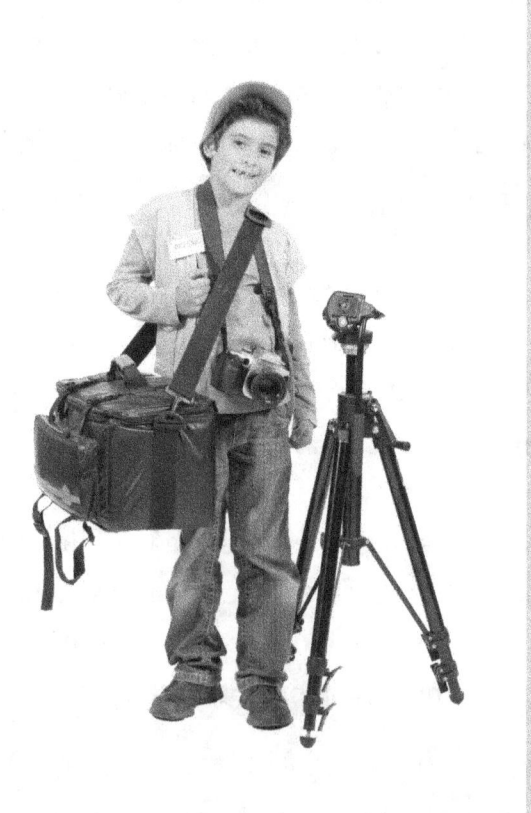

Someday, you'll get to look back at what you wrote and get a "snapshot" of you in the Wild.

SCRAPBOOK PICTURES

*Glue a couple pictures here
to remember your Activity*

You can keep the pictures in Your Family Wild Activity book, your own Scrapbook, or put them in a frame to commemorate your activities years from now!

Below-take a few minutes and tell your ACTIVITY STORY.
In your own words. Think of it as telling the story to your Grandchildren some day! Do it in your own words and handwriting-like your sending a post card to someone 50-100 years from now!

Our Family Wild Activity Story

_____

_____

_____

_____

_____

_____

Family Wild

> "Help others reach their dreams and you will achieve yours."
>
> Les Brown
> **American Author**

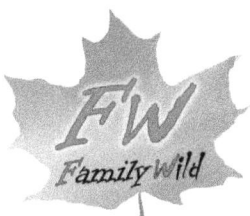
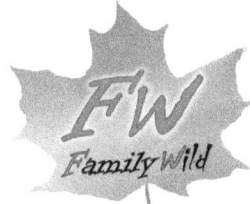

Personalize Your Life Preserver

Objective: Make your life preserver easy to identify and more fun to wear.

What You Might Need:

Fabric paint or Derwent Intense Color blocks

Newspaper or plastic table cloth

Jar of water

Rag

Several paint brushes

Sharpie marker

Drawing paper

pencil

Transfer paper **(graphite paper)**

Life preserver

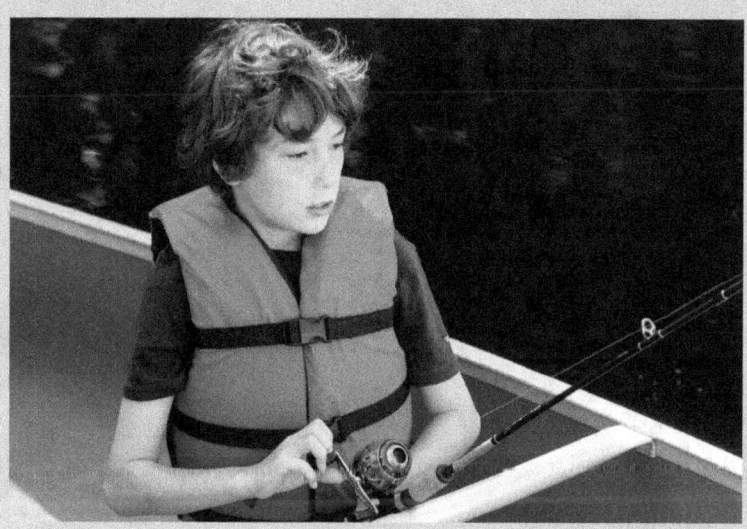

Jump In!

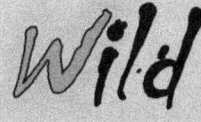 **QUOTE** *"Art takes nature as its model."*

Aristotle

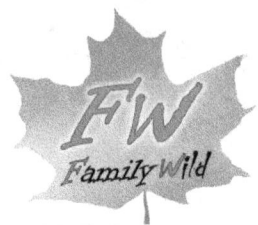

Whenever you are fishing on rough terrain, or in a boat, be sure you use a life preserver.

This protective device isn't a statement about how well you swim - it's a safety net if you hit your head or are too hurt to get your head above the water.

The best lesson about nature is to expect the unexpected. Yeah, most of life preservers out there are kind of boring, but imagine painting your vest to make it your own! What colors do you love? What statement do you want to make on the water? Let's get started!

First, get your life preserver. Be sure it fits correctly and is designed for your weight. Look at it carefully and imagine what image you would like on it...or maybe a special set of words or your name in fancy letters is more your style.

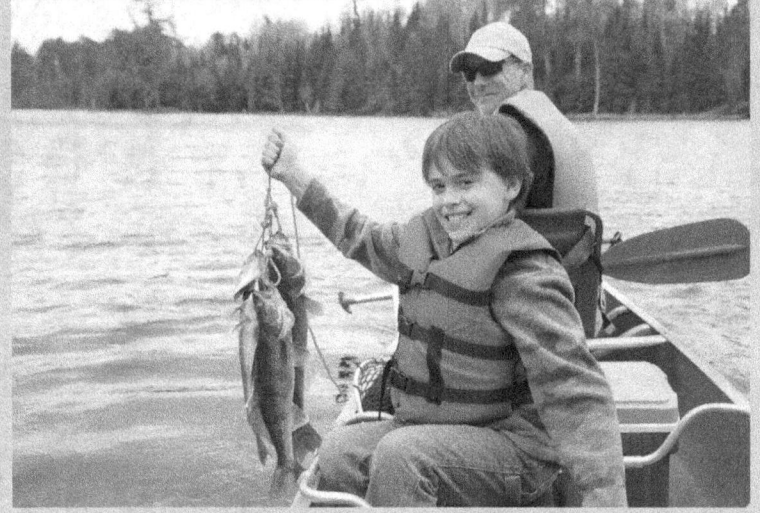

If you don't trust your hand, you can actually use stencils bought from an arts and craft store, or by copying an image with tracing paper and then transferring it onto your preserver with the graphite paper. Another thing you can do is draw your image freehand with a Sharpie waterproof pen and then paint in the design. Be creative!

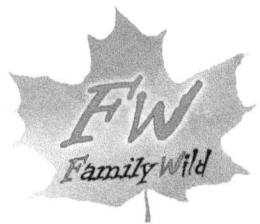

Next, lay out a cloth or newspaper to protect the surface where you are working. Gather your paint brushes, paints, water and cloth. If you are using the color blocks, they are all you need for the coloring. Either draw or transfer the image you have chosen to create onto the life preserver. Give a few minutes for the ink to dry if you are using a Sharpie pen.

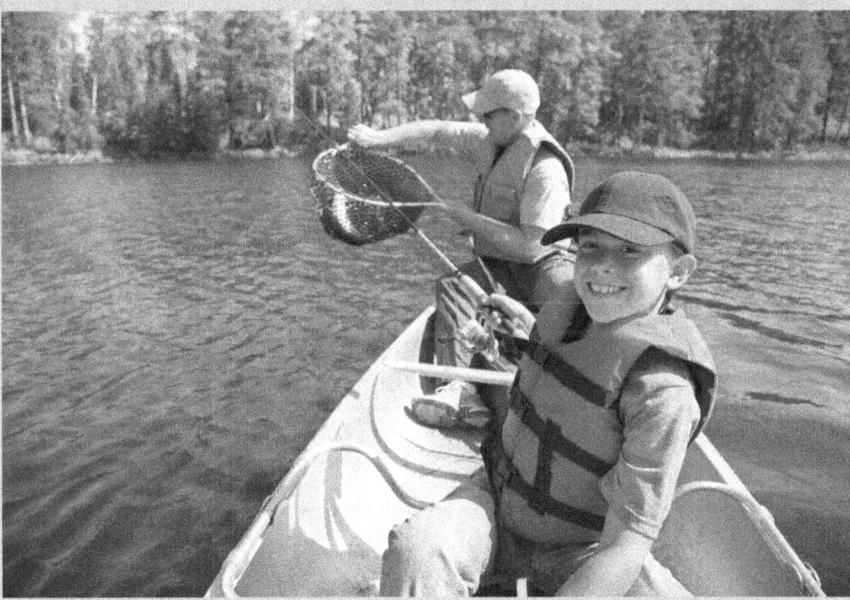

For stencils, tape the stencil in place and using a very fat and squat brush, dab the paint into the cut-out image. For color blocks, you can shade in the stencil areas, and even add several colors for more interest in each part of your design.

When you are done, give your project a day to dry completely. Be sure to clean up carefully, recapping all the paints and ink pens or storing the ink blocks in their container.

Now you can be your Wild self on the water-and be safe, too.

SCRAPBOOK PICTURES

*Glue a couple pictures here
to remember your Activity*

You can keep the pictures in Your Family Wild Activity book, your own Scrapbook, or put them in a frame to commemorate your activities years from now!

Below-take a few minutes and tell your ACTIVITY STORY. In your own words. Think of it as telling the story to your Grandchildren some day! Do it in your own words and handwriting-like your sending a post card to someone 50-100 years from now!

Our Family Wild Activity Story

_____

_____

_____

_____

_____

_____

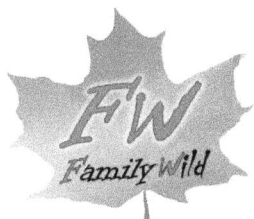 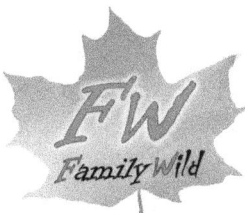

Music in the Wild

Objective: Using found objects, as well as basic percussion or simple woodwinds such Native American flutes, to express the moods of nature.

What You Might Need:

Natural objects
Rocks, hand sized
Two pieces of dried wood
Handful of dried leaves
Pine cones

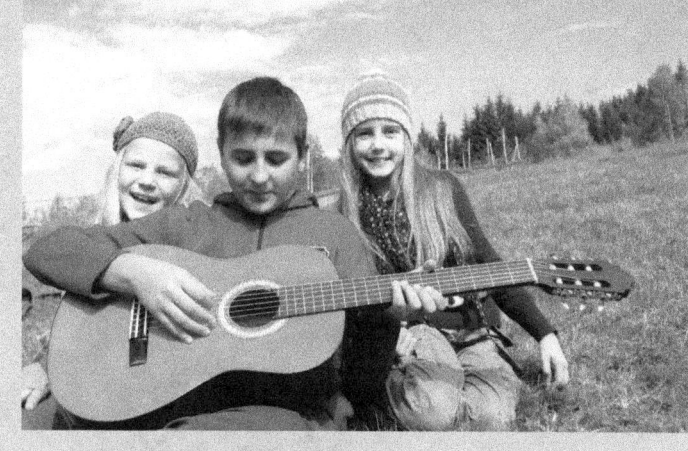

Drums or home-made percussion instruments like a cooking bowl turned upside down, milk jug with a little gravel or dried beans (tape the top closed), small plastic storage containers with seeds, dried rice or even buttons -tape up the container, or two wooden spoons.

Wooden flute, penny whistle, recorder, or other easy to carry instrument you may play

Jump in!

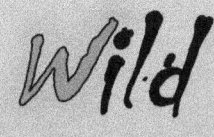

QUOTE

"Art will never be able to exist without nature."

Pierre Bonnard

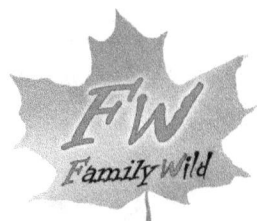

One of the most magical times around a campfire happened when a few college friends decided to make music. One of us had a Native American flute but nobody else had any other man made instrument! So, we hit the forest, picking up rocks, sticks, pine cones, even handfuls of dried leaves and grasses.

We gathered back together and the music we made was like the forest itself singing. The flute picked up a steady, low melody and we just began to add to it - rocks clicking together, the sticks clacking in time, the dried leaves scrunching and muttering.

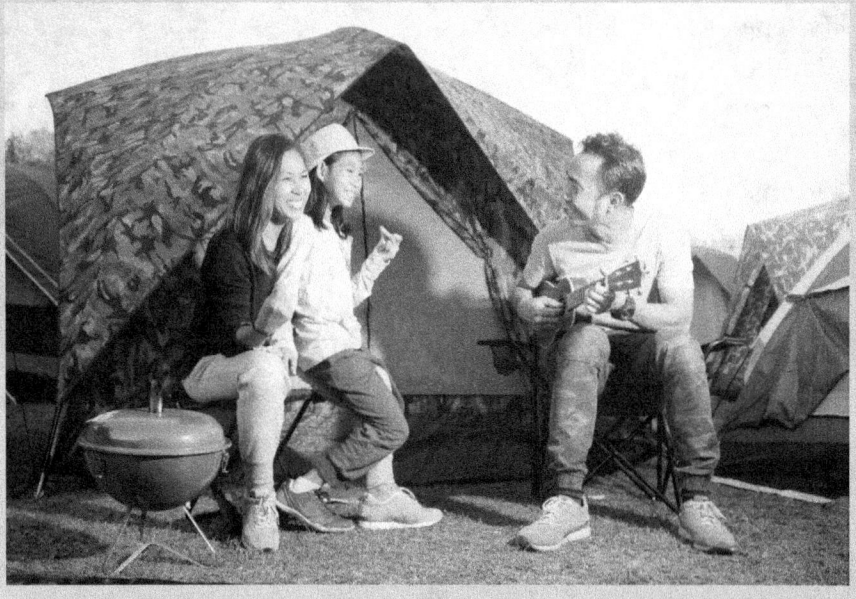

Music isn't just on the radio or at the concert! And it isn't about a recording contract or You Tube hit. We live surrounded by music-it's hiding in our cooking bowls and wooden spoons, in our table tops and the way we can slap our hands together, it's in the birdsongs we try to copy by whistling,

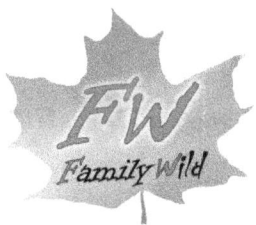

the way the bass splashes up against the boat, the mysterious whisper of the wind moving through leaves. Music is a language, an invitation to a conversation-and you don't need to be a musician to join.

So take what you have at hand or go out into the woods and fields and find your instruments. Gather your family in the yard or living-room or on the pontoon boat or around that campfire. And just make sounds together.

Laugh! Take pictures! Or better, make a little video recording of your music! Go Wild!

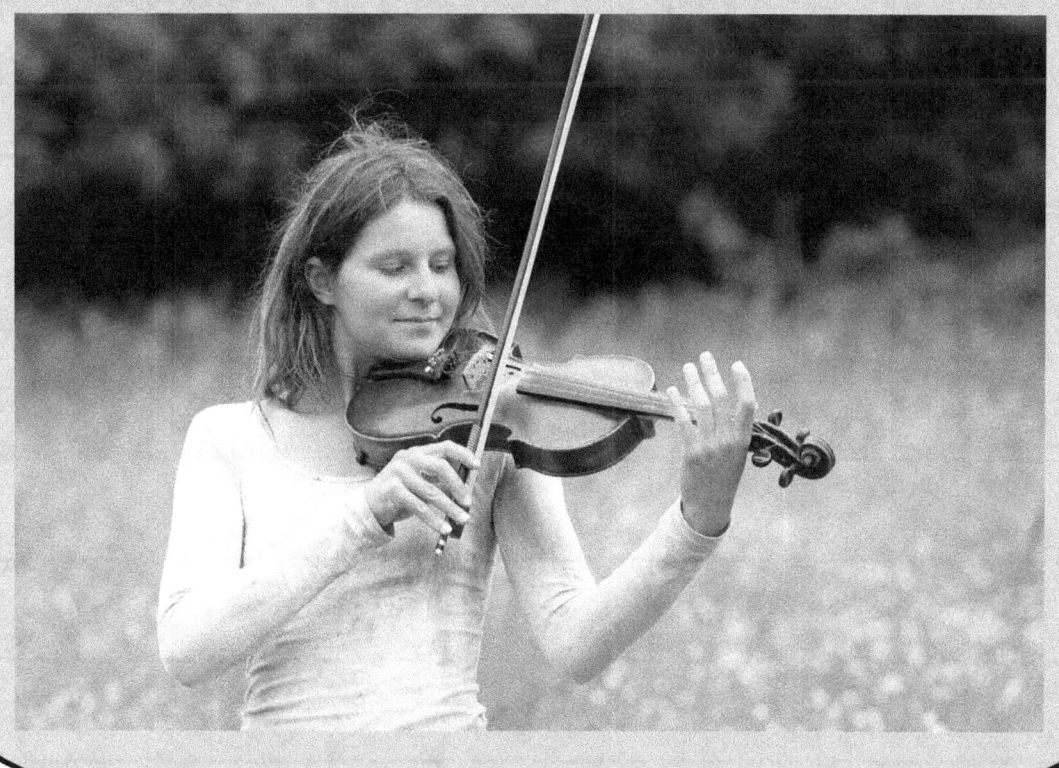

SCRAPBOOK PICTURES

*Glue a couple pictures here
to remember your Activity*

You can keep the pictures in Your Family Wild Activity book,
your own Scrapbook, or put them in a frame
to commemorate your activities years from now!

Below-take a few minutes and tell your ACTIVITY STORY.
In your own words. Think of it as telling the story to
your Grandchildren some day! Do it in your own words
and handwriting-like your sending a post card to
someone 50-100 years from now!

Our Family Wild Activity Story

_____

_____

_____

_____

_____

_____

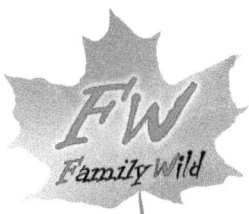
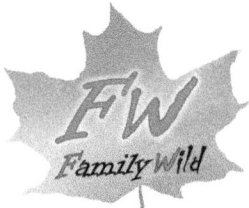

Painting Wildlife

Objective: Create simple artwork using acrylics and graphite paper to transfer wildlife images to the canvas.

What You Might Need:

Sketching paper
Graphite paper - light and dark
Tape
Trash bags
Heavy #6 pencil for transferring images
Canvas or canvas board
Variety of brushes
Basic acrylic paint set
Plastic plate for mixing colors
Rags

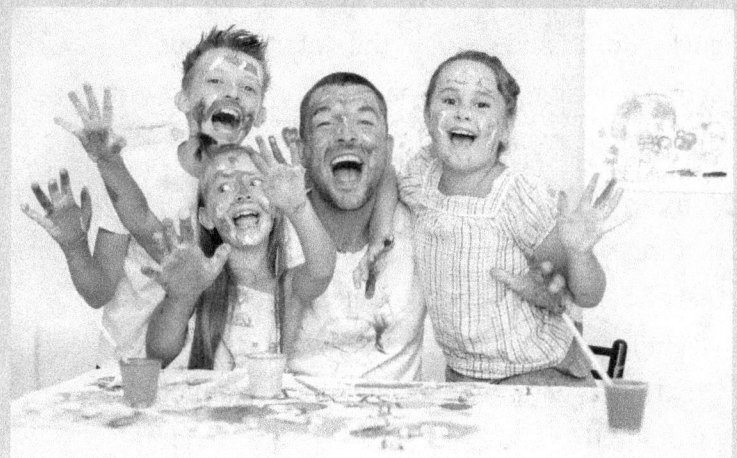

Images of animals-look in old calendars, on the internet, photos you have taken, etc.

Images of natural settings or even bring the real material inside
Work table or easel

Jump in!

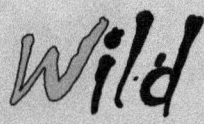

QUOTE

"Because the landscape has always been an integral part of my life, I have developed a deep sense of belonging to nature rather than feeling apart from it or above it."

Clyde Aspevig

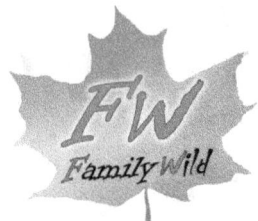

Painting your own wildlife pictures can be a lot of fun. Many folks balk at the idea "I can't even draw!" But with the internet and a decent printer, you can actually find images you like, size them up or down to fit your canvas and then print them off. By changing the backgrounds and some of the details in your actual painting, you will have a work that is your own unique expression.

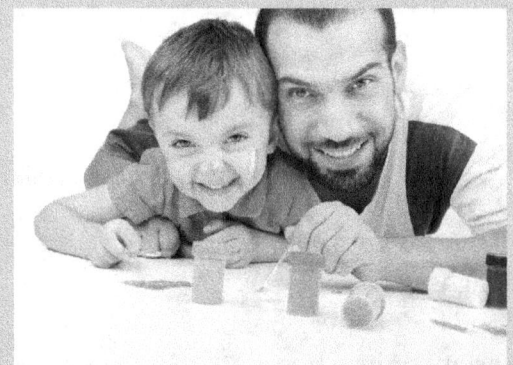

You can also collect images - old calendars, pictures you have taken, old picture books from used bookstores or garage sales. These snapshots will help you with the details in your painting. Create files with the different kinds of animals or plant life that you like to paint to refer to later.

Consider bringing in dried grasses, twigs, fresh flowers and what have you - these real materials can also help you learn to see colors and textures that might not be apparent in flat pictures of these items.

Set up a workspace - it can be as simple as a card-table. Protect the surface of your table and the floor with split-open trash bags. You can use an old spaghetti jar to hold your brushes and another to hold your water for quick-cleaning. Keep some rags or paper toweling at hand to help with clean ups and spills.

First, paint in your background. When you are first learning, it's easiest to do "studies" - a bird on a simple branch, a deer head with a fuzzy background, etc. Squeeze out a few colors and blend them on your plate - remember, this is play! You can find color wheels and other color blending books on the internet or at your local library if you want more pointers.

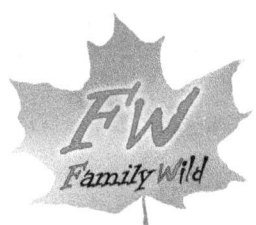

Once the background is completed, let it dry for a full day. Then, take the image of the animal and tape it with one small strip on your canvas. Using the graphite paper (light color for dark backgrounds or dark graphite for light backgrounds) and a #6 hard pencil, transfer the image over to the canvas (just slide the paper under your image and trace the image with the pencil). You can also do this with images you have drawn yourself! Remove the image and the graphite paper and you will be able to see a faint outline of the animal you will be painting.

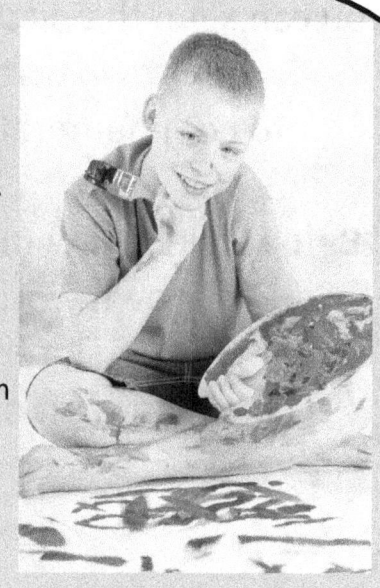

Using all the pictures you have assembled of your animal, fill in the details. If you have access to the internet, there are some excellent You Tube videos that will show you how to use light, paint textures and other techniques. Be sure to visit our blog- we try to keep at least a few good links for each chapter in our books for you to explore and we will eventually have a short video to support every chapter in our books, created with our family and friends. But always remember: looking at books and videos is not the real thing. The best part of painting is to experiment with a deep sense of play.

If you have small children, they still will love painting images you have transferred onto canvas or heavy-stock paper. Acrylics clean up very easily and dry much faster than oil paints.

Don't fear the paint!

Remember - you are Wild!

SCRAPBOOK PICTURES

*Glue a couple pictures here
to remember your Activity*

You can keep the pictures in Your Family Wild Activity book,
your own Scrapbook, or put them in a frame
to commemorate your activities years from now!

Below-take a few minutes and tell your ACTIVITY STORY.
In your own words. Think of it as telling the story to
your Grandchildren some day! Do it in your own words
and handwriting-like your sending a post card to
someone 50-100 years from now!

Our Family Wild Activity Story

_____

_____

_____

_____

_____

_____

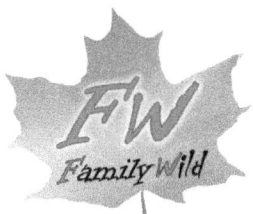
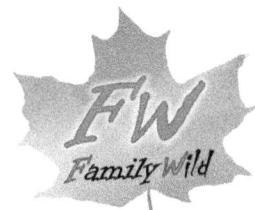

Drawing Wildlife

Objective: Work with pencils to capture black and white wildlife images.

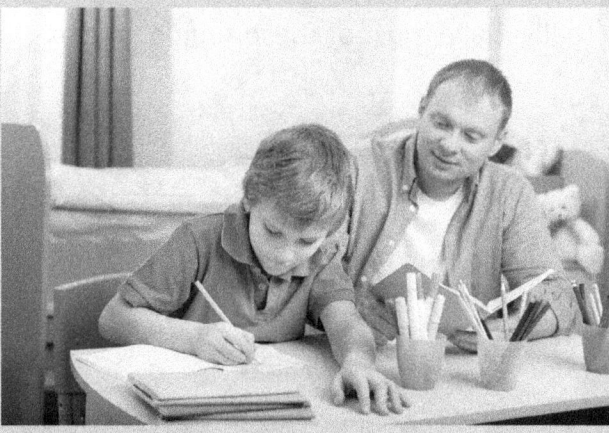

What You Might Need:

Drawing pencil

Fine-tipped Sharpie pens

Drawing paper or Sketch book

Graphite paper: dark

Collection of wildlife images from photos, old calendars, old picture books

Computer, printer and scanner (optional)

Jump in!

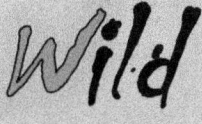

QUOTE

"Knowing trees, I understand the meaning of patience. Knowing grass, I can appreciate persistence."

Hal Borland

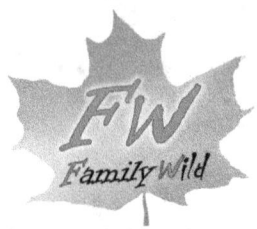

Right off the bat, don't think of this as "making ART"- rather, consider your first attempts at drawing as pure fun. In the bookstores right now are tons of "adult coloring books". Did you know you can actually make most of these simple images yourself?

First, gather some pictures that you really like - they may be photographs cut out from magazines, pictures from the internet, or even images you have captured on your smartphone. Select one to start with.

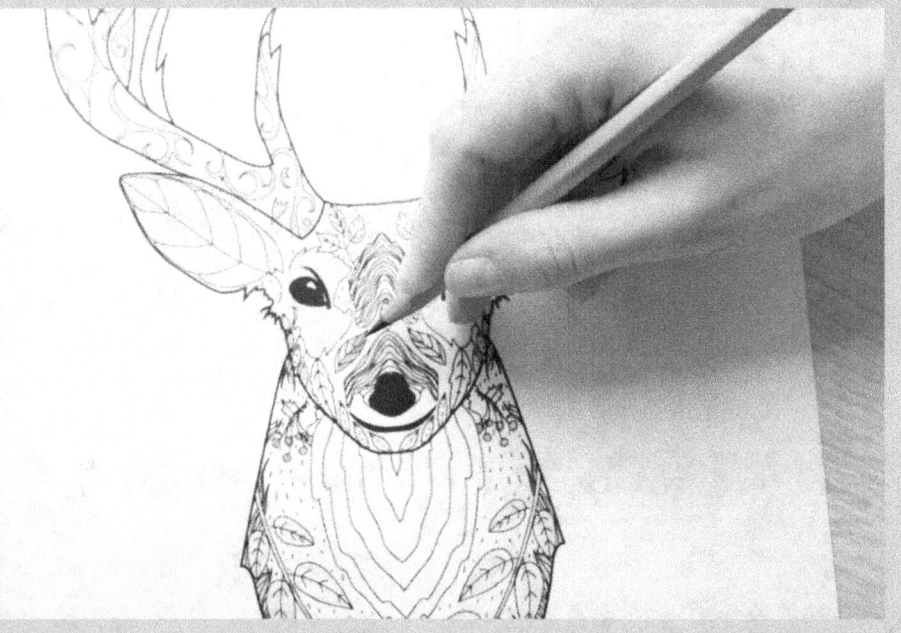

Now, look deeply at the picture. Where does your eye go first - the curve of the ram horn, the outstretched neck of the goose, mystery of the hummingbird's wings, all blurred and full of motion, the diamonds of a flower petal?

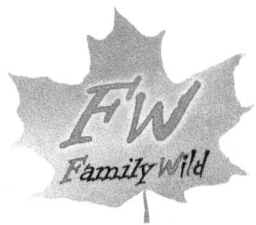

Study that focal point-what geometric shape would best fit it? For instance, the ram horn would fit well in a half-moon shape, the goose neck looks like an elongated oval with a smaller oval for the head, the hummingbird wings combine arcs and straight lines back to the body.

Using a soft pencil, try to capture that geometry on your paper. Erase any mistakes and start again. You can also put copy paper over your image (be sure it is enlarged enough to play with) and lightly sketch the shape - triangle, oval, circle, etc.) Continue to add geometry to create your full picture, studying each part of the animal piece by piece.

For example, the legs of many animals are like long tubes, heads can have both circular and triangular elements (like the beak of a partridge). It looks really cool to not connect the different shapes - your eye will actually make the different elements work together!

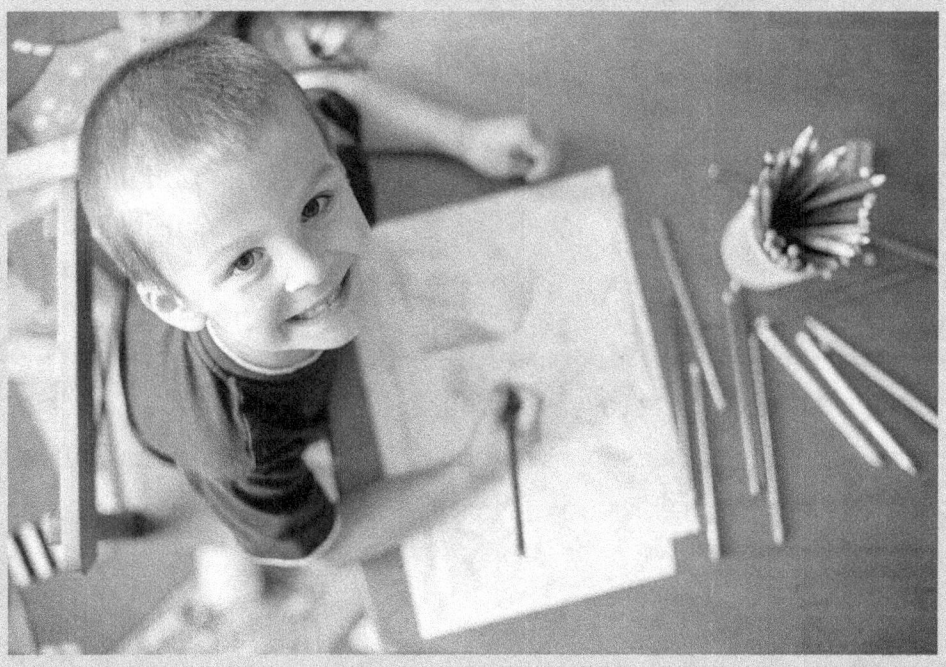

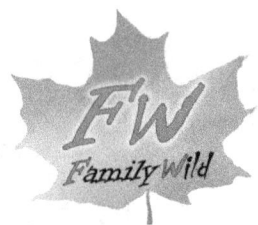

Now, carefully ink in the geometric shape. You could have images like these:

Using these building blocks, add in interesting swoops, lines, paisley images, etc. that can easily be colored in. Your image now will look something like this:

Over time, create ten or more images that you can scan and copy together to create your own coloring book or make one for a gift for a both adults or kids! You can also copy your pictures using copy paper and then transfer the image 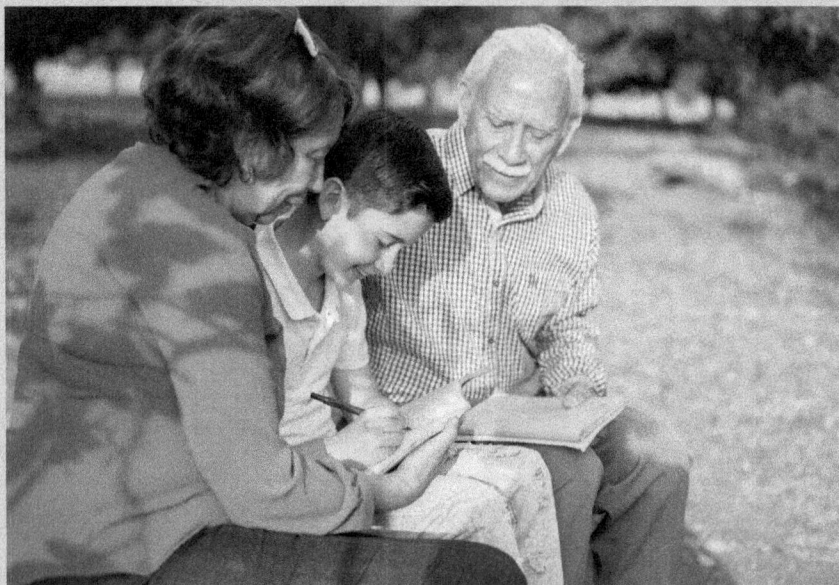 to flower pots, pictures frames, glass - use the graphite paper to move the image to the new project. Paint in the images to make beautiful crafts.

Please do send Family Wild any of the drawings that turn out really well and we'll feature them on our blog! (You can find how to submit ideas, photographs, recipes and more and win great prizes in the appendix of this book.) No artist is too young - we love seeing your Wild work!

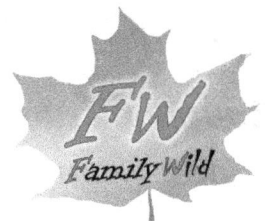

Kim's Examples

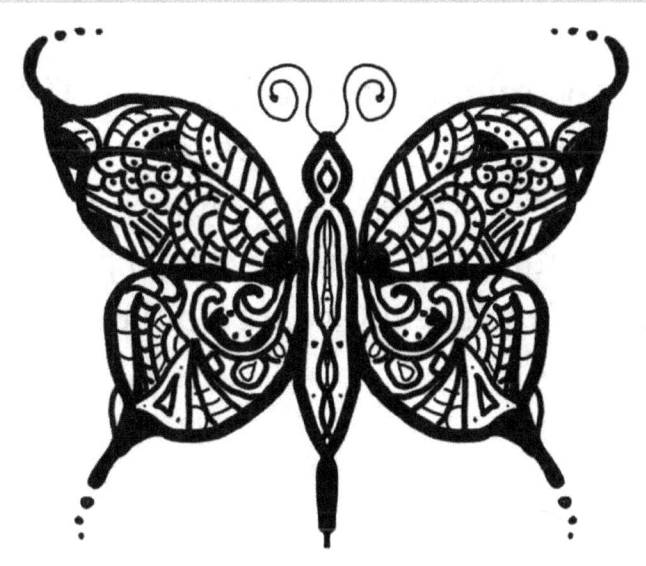

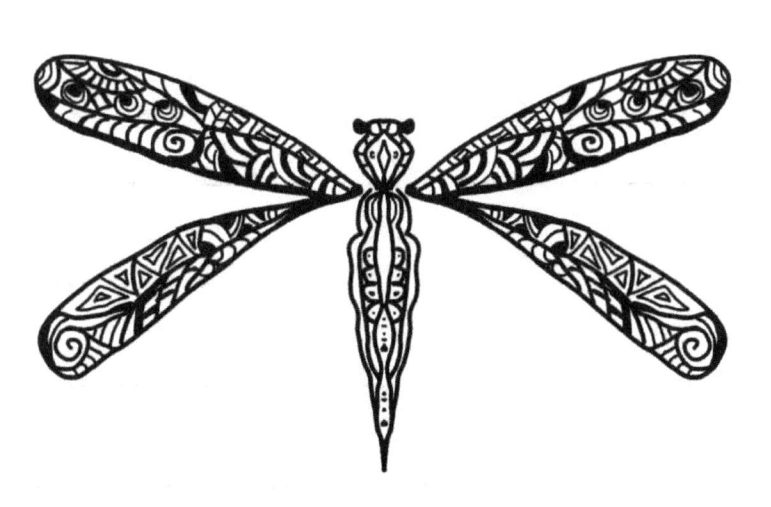

SCRAPBOOK PICTURES

Glue a couple pictures here
to remember your Activity

You can keep the pictures in Your Family Wild Activity book,
your own Scrapbook, or put them in a frame
to commemorate your activities years from now!

Below-take a few minutes and tell your ACTIVITY STORY.
In your own words. Think of it as telling the story to
your Grandchildren some day! Do it in your own words
and handwriting-like your sending a post card to
someone 50-100 years from now!

Our Family Wild Activity Story

_____

_____

_____

_____

_____

_____

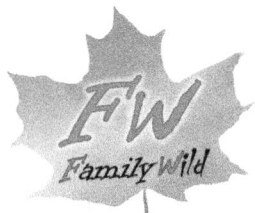
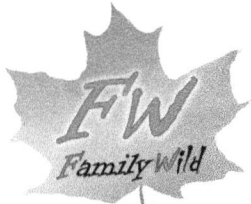

Sculpting Wildlife

Objective: learn to appreciate animals in three dimensions, by creating sculptures that follow muscular and skeletal lines.

What You Might Need:

Sculpey clay in a plain tan, brown or terra cotta color or a self-hardening clay

Newspapers or plastic tablecloth

Simple tools like toothpicks, large nails, etc. to add detail
Cookie bake sheet covered with aluminum foil

Oven

Picture of animal to sculpt, with several poses. They need not be the same animal, but try to stay true to the age and general shape of what you are trying to create.

Jump in!

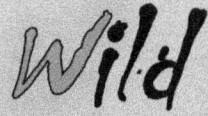

QUOTE

"At the end of the day, Mother Nature has only one question for us: 'What life did you nurture today?"

Robert Brault

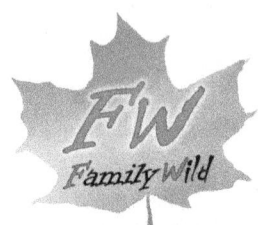

Sculpting can be a great deal of fun on a snowy afternoon. Try to use a brand of clay like Sculpey, which can be baked in your own oven or a self-hardening clay. Lay out newspapers or a plastic table cloth to protect the surface you are working on.

You can actually built and detail your sculpture on a baking tray covered with aluminum foil so you don't have to shift the finished work when it is time to bake it.

You might enjoy working with a critter built a little more "close to the ground" like a squirrel, turtle or raccoon. Gather all the pictures of the animal together. It helps to have close-ups of the feet, face, fur patterns or shell-shapes.

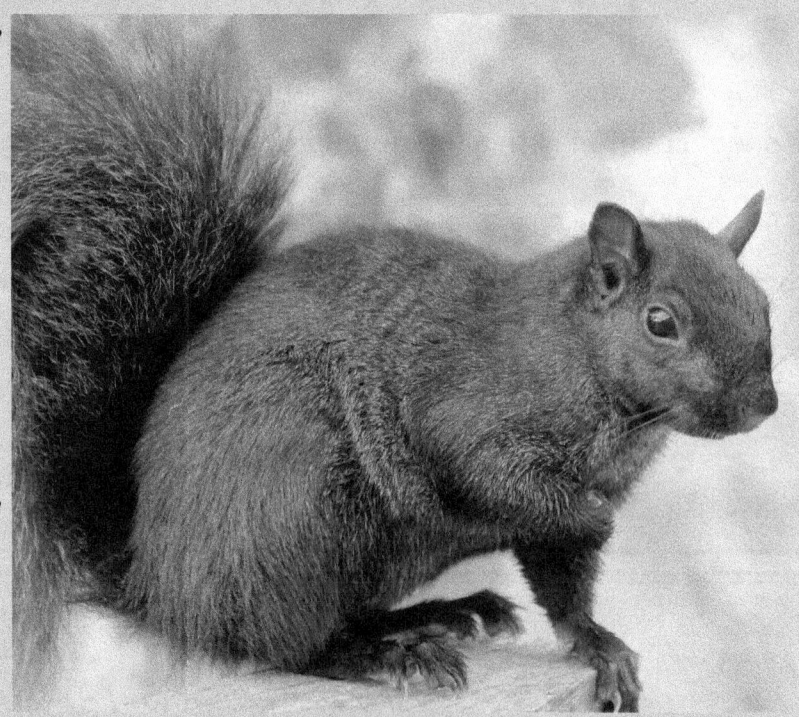

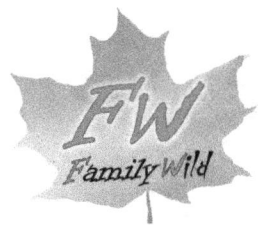

Next, look at the basic geometry of the animal. Is the head more like a ball or sort of like a triangle? What shapes do you see in the legs? The neck? The body? The tail?

You can actually start by creating these simple shapes, then carefully connect all the pieces until you have a rough shape of the animal.

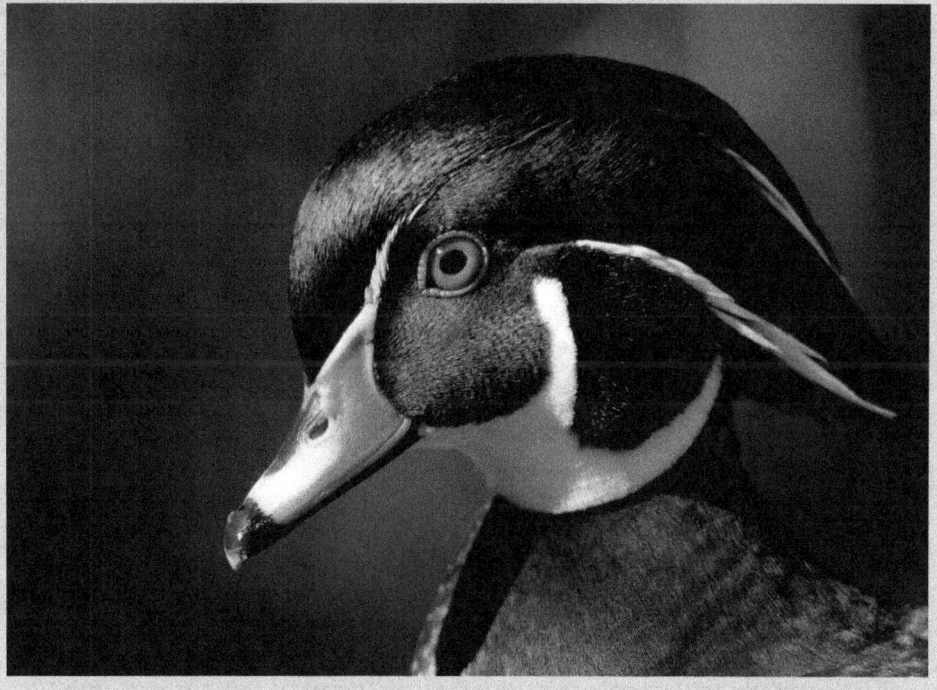

At this stage, look the sculpture over, and make any corrections you need to - maybe the head could use a little more clay or one of the legs is too long. Be sure to get the basic shapes right.

Then smooth out the areas where you have connected the various shapes.

When you are done, the head, neck, body, ears, legs or wings or shell, and tail should all flow together without obvious join lines.

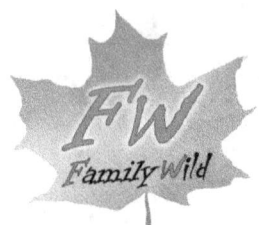

Now you are ready to add the details. Look carefully at the pictures so you can place the eyes, hollow out the ears, detail in claws, etc.

The fun thing about clay is that if you make a mistake, you can smooth it out and start again.

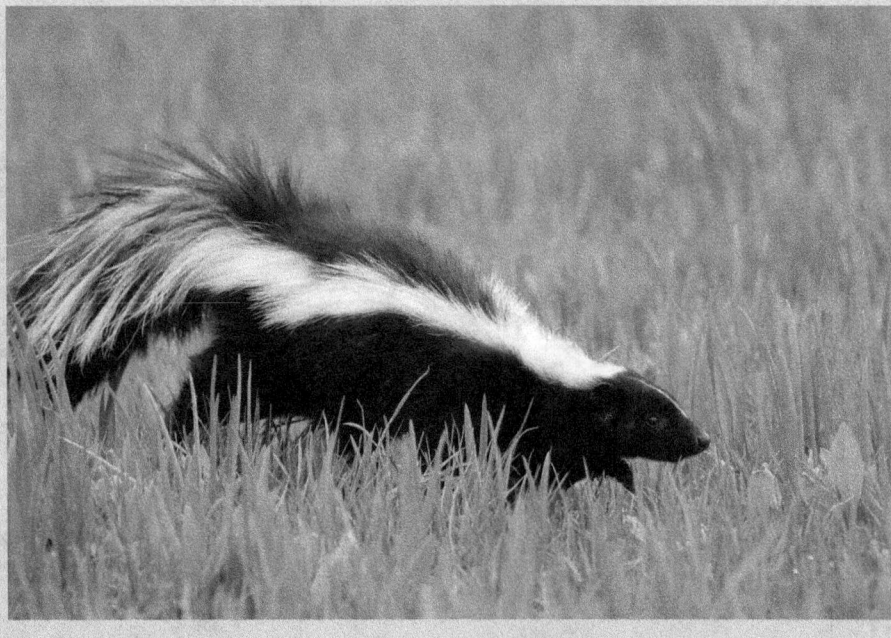

Work small and close and take your time. If you need to take a break, you should cover self-hardening clay with a damp cloth.

Sculpey stays relatively workable until you bake it.

Once you are happy with your sculpture, you can follow the package instructions to bake Sculpey. If you are using self-hardening clay, set the animal aside until the clay has set up fully. You've explored one more way to link your own creativity with the Wild.

SCRAPBOOK PICTURES

Glue a couple pictures here
to remember your Activity

You can keep the pictures in Your Family Wild Activity book,
your own Scrapbook, or put them in a frame
to commemorate your activities years from now!

Below-take a few minutes and tell your ACTIVITY STORY.
In your own words. Think of it as telling the story to
your Grandchildren some day! Do it in your own words
and handwriting-like your sending a post card to
someone 50-100 years from now!

Our Family Wild Activity Story

_____

_____

_____

_____

_____

_____

Family Wild

> "If you see something that moves you, and then snap it, you keep a moment."
>
> Linda McCartney
> **Photographer**

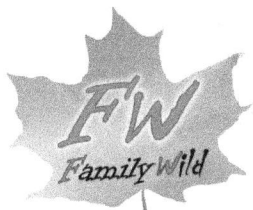
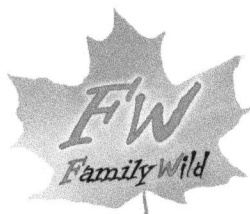

Wildlife Photography

"Mike here. Kim was kind enough to let me write this activity. I owned two professional photography studios for twelve years and taught photography at our local community college for nine years. If you love photography, watch for our Family Wild Photography book coming soon!" — M. W. Nunneley

Objective: Learn to "Paint" with light as you photograph a wilderness scene several times of the day, different days, different months and through out the year.

What You Might Need:

A Camera. Any camera. One of the best kept secrets in photography is that the cost or quality of your camera isn't as big a deal as you think. In fact, for this activity, the camera on your phone will work!

A Computer, Printer or Photo Lab -

I recommend you use a digital camera for this project to keep costs down and allow you to take a lot of photos. Again your phone will work or a simple digital or film camera. You will need some way to see your photos. Print then one's you like.

A Favorite Outdoor Scene - Pick an interesting outdoor scene. Try and I look for wooded area, a stream, a path or a field. Really, pick somewhere you LOVE to visit.

A Tripod (Optional but recommended)

String or ribbon

Jump in!

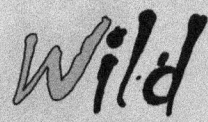

QUOTE

"Not enough fishing, the problem is."

Yoda

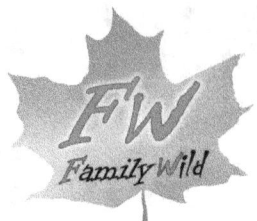

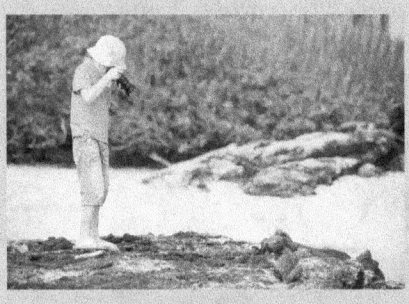

When I taught photography to college students, we'd start out talking about painting— painting with light! As a photographer, you need to train your eye to see how "light" looks to your camera.

When you look at something, your magical eyes "filter" many sights on the way to your brain. This activity is designed to show you how your camera sees. Your camera see indiscriminately. In other words, a camera sees everything and consequently captures everything.

With camera in hand, I want you to pick out your favorite spot outdoors. Try and find an interesting place. In other words, if you love a certain woods, find a favorite path. If you like a river, find the most visually interesting part of the river. Make sure you like this spot as you're going to visit it often!

Once you've found your heaven on earth place, mark you spot with a ribbon or string on a tree or rock. You're going to do this so you can come back to the exact spot over the rest of the day, the next week, or all year!

If you're really motivated, I want you to get up before dark and get to your spot with your camera. Literally dark, as if you were hunting. You may want to pick your deer blind as your magical photography spot. As the light comes up, start taking pictures. If you have a tripod, use it. Put your camera on automatic settings for the activity, you want to make everything automatic except for your light!

For the first hour of light, take as many photos as you want. At minimum, take one every 5 - 10 minutes. Once you've taken all the photos you want in the morning, pack it up until 11 am. Try NOT to look at your photos until the end of the day. I know it will be hard in the digital age, but when I was a photographer, we had to send off all our film and wait anywhere from an hour to a week to see our pictures!

Now pack a lunch and head back to your spot. Try and get as close to exactly where you were this morning. Once you're ready, do the same thing all over again! Take all the photos you want and make sure you take at least one every five minutes. Once you've had your fill take this time to photograph other things out in the woods. Have fun - click away!

Remember how I said make sure you love this spot? That's because I want you to

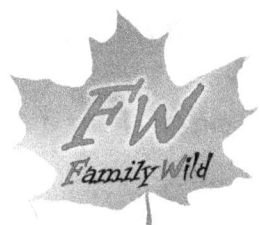

head back an hour before sunset. Same as before, set up as close to the same spot as you did at lunch and sunrise. You know the drill, take as many photos as you want. Again, make sure you get at least one every five to ten minutes and hold off your urge to look. Think of it like Christmas Morning! Once you're done, pack up and head to your computer. I know you can "look" on your phone or camera but you'll see the detail better on your computer.

Once home, download your photos and look at what you've "painted! Take special note of the direction of the light. Watch how the highlighted lights look in comparison to the shadows.

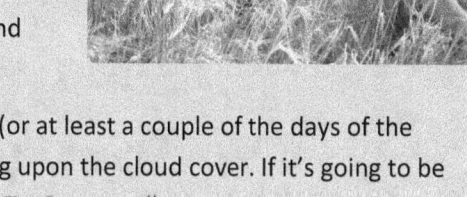

Which time of day created photos you like better? What "light" looked really awesome. I call it "cool" light. What parts looked dreary and dead?

Now for the real over achievers, do this for the rest of the week (or at least a couple of the days of the rest of the week.) Each day should look quite different depending upon the cloud cover. If it's going to be totally sunny or totally cloudy wait and pick a very different day. Try for a totally sunny day, a partly cloudy day, an overcast day and a really dark day. Check out the differences.

One of the most amazing photographic series I've ever seen was a man whose house sat on the southwest side of Michigan's Mackinaw Bridge. For one year, every day, this man photographed Mighty Mac. The differences in the images was stunning and he NEVER moved his camera from its place on the tripod facing his front window.

If you have the time and dedication, try going back to your favorite place every month or at least every season. What differences do you see in your photo's from the Spring to Summer to Winter and Fall. Try and go the same time of the day to keep your experiment consistent.

Feel free to put people, pets or other subjects "in" your photographs. Watch how the light falls on them. See if you like the highlights on their hair or face. Pose them if you want, turn them, have fun with it!

If you want some further variety, get low to the ground or high in the sky, like in a tree blind, and try the same activity from a different height perspective. You might also find one tree, or limb or rock to focus upon as your actual "subject." If you get some fun photos and enjoyed this activity, submit them to Family Wild and we'll take a look at them!

SCRAPBOOK PICTURES

*Glue a couple pictures here
to remember your Activity*

You can keep the pictures in Your Family Wild Activity book,
your own Scrapbook, or put them in a frame
to commemorate your activities years from now!

Below-take a few minutes and tell your ACTIVITY STORY.
In your own words. Think of it as telling the story to
your Grandchildren some day! Do it in your own words
and handwriting-like your sending a post card to
someone 50-100 years from now!

Our Family Wild Activity Story

_____

_____

_____

_____

_____

_____

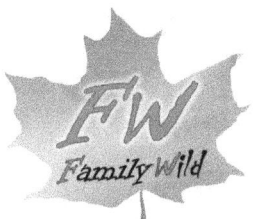
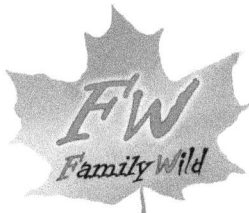

Wildlife Blogs & Facebook

Objective: Create a Facebook Page or personal blog to share your experiences in nature and connect to other folks in your area or across the world.

What you might need:

Access to a computer

Access to the internet

Digital camera or

Smartphone that allows you to Upload pictures you take

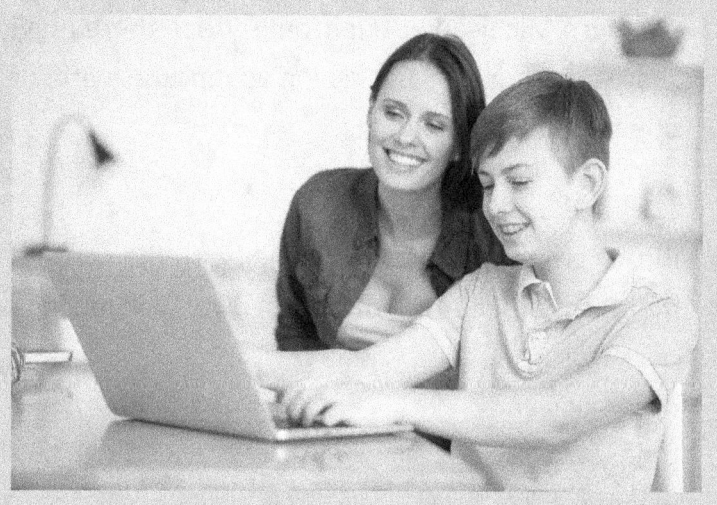

Domain name purchase to boost your blog - usually around $12.00.

Jump in!

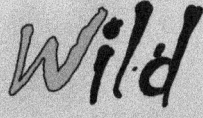

QUOTE

"As the woods are the same, the trees standing in their places, the rocks and the earth...they are always different too, as lights and shadows and seasons and moods pass through them."

Emily Carr

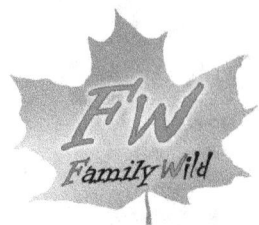

Sometimes, depending on where you live, you may be bursting with great photos and experiences to share and not have a lot of folks around that "get" you.

Maybe you are living with your mom in a big city, or your family owns a farm in northern Michigan - aside from school, there may not be many other kids close by to share your hunting and fishing adventures with, or a place to show off your latest poem, recipe or painting.

But by creating a Facebook page (with the consent and help from your adult family members or your friend/mentor), you will have a way to reach out to others, hear back from other kids and teens who like what you like, and best of all, keep some of your best work on the web where it is safe from fires, floods and dropped laptop damages!

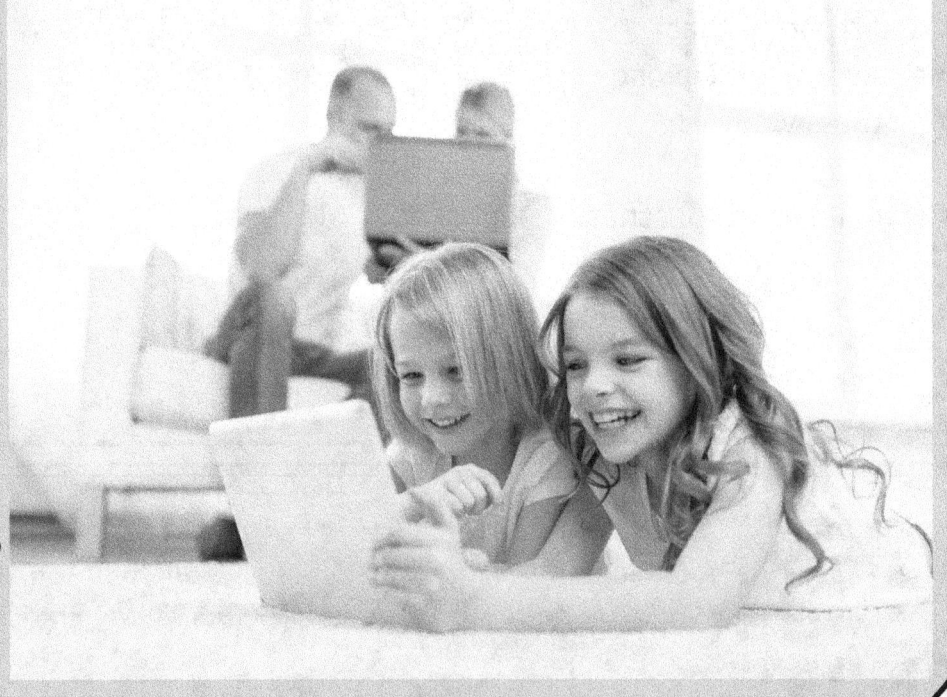

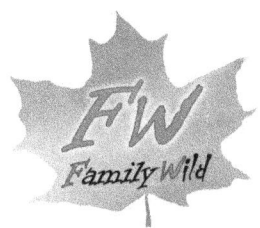

Before you begin creating either a blog or a Facebook page, here are some things to get in place -

Come up with a really great and unusual name for your blog or Page - something that tells folks what your site is about without being boring! The more unique you make it, the easier it is to claim a domain name or make your page stand on Facebook.

Decide ahead of time how much your family is willing to spend online. This is really important because comments on blogs and messages about your page can eat up the clock really fast. Don't let this activity keep you from the best part of your life...Living WILD!

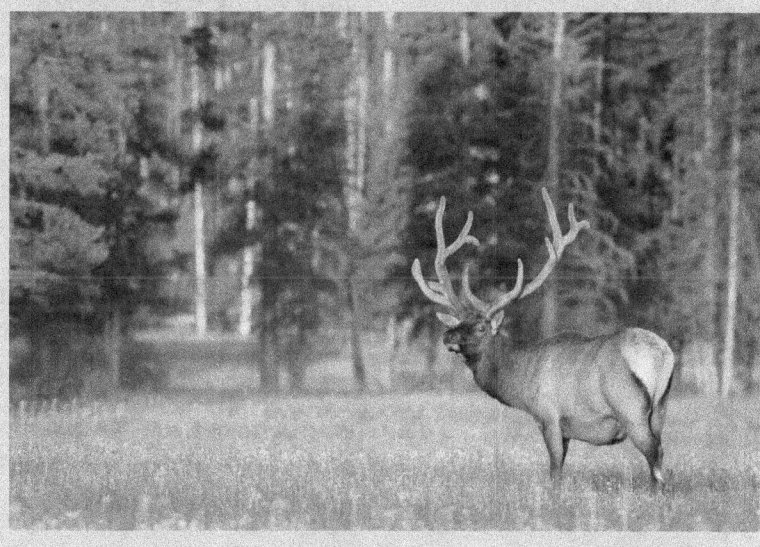

Learn how to transfer photos from your phone or camera to your computer. Pictures add so much color and interest to what you are writing. You can also use "public domain" images on your blog and Facebook page. Learn more about this in the resources section of this chapter.

Identify cool things you want to share that maybe you've already written about or created, like pictures of that huge perch you caught, or a short clip of the family music making activity, or an MP3 recording of learning to use a turkey call. All that stuff is great material for your internet site.

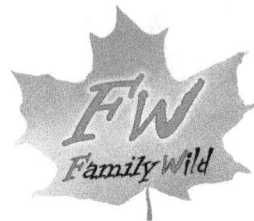

Take the time to watch the instructional videos listed in the resource section - they'll get you on your way to making a really cool site. If it's a blog you're interested in writing (and parents, blogs are great because they are often more "hidden" than a Facebook page and you can shut off the "comment" section on a blog) be sure to read and follow the directions about how to create your blog on the site you select.

Create a link to Family Wild's Facebook page and blog or website - this will connect you with others Wild folk and give you a lot of chances to make friends and share cool ideas.

A blog or Page can be a kind of internet journal - the sky is the limit for posting. You can learn how to link your blog to You Tube so you can upload your own digital video productions, scan in your artwork, post your poetry and recipes, keep track of how weather in your area affects your hunting and fishing - the list is endless.

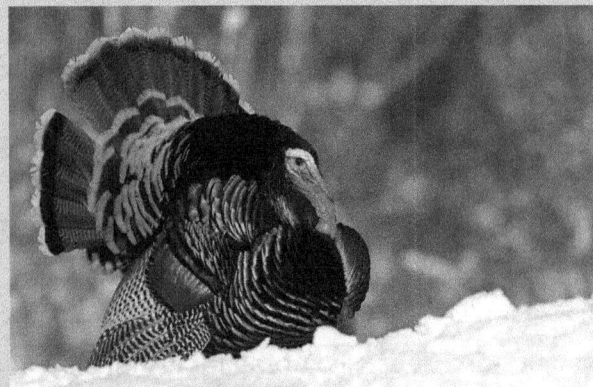

And you can access it pretty easily from anywhere, in this age of the smartphone. For those of you who love to write and may be thinking about a career in writing, marketing, wildlife research, professional art and more, this activity will help you start to get your voice out there! So post WILD!

SCRAPBOOK PICTURES

Glue a couple pictures here
to remember your Activity

You can keep the pictures in Your Family Wild Activity book,
your own Scrapbook, or put them in a frame
to commemorate your activities years from now!

Below-take a few minutes and tell your ACTIVITY STORY.
In your own words. Think of it as telling the story to
your Grandchildren some day! Do it in your own words
and handwriting-like your sending a post card to
someone 50-100 years from now!

Our Family Wild Activity Story

_____

_____

_____

_____

_____

_____

Family Wild

"I'm a big illustration and comic book fan. In my eyes, comic books and illustration are the same kind of art forms."

Mika
British Musician

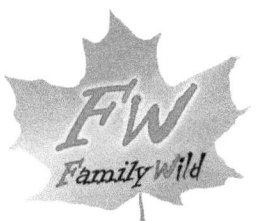
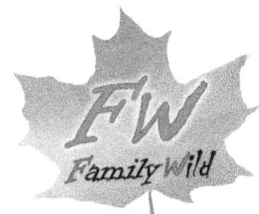

Outdoor Comic Design

Objectives: Exploring the visual impact of words with basic line drawing or color as well as learning to fine tune the ability to recognize, appreciate and share humorous tales about nature.

What You Might Need:

Paper

Pen or pencil

Ruler

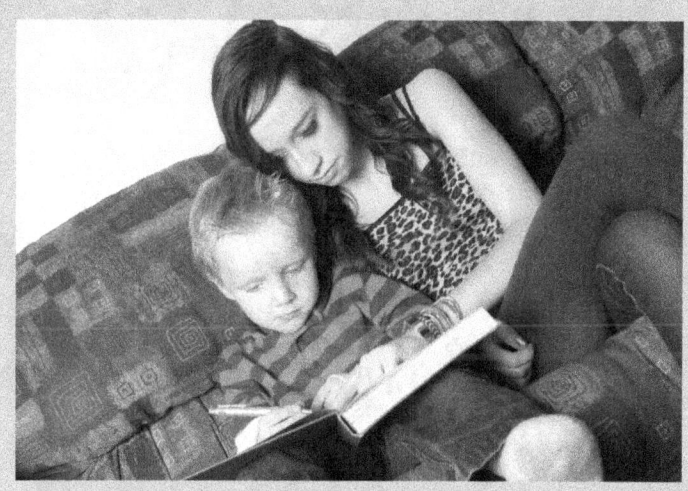

Jump in!

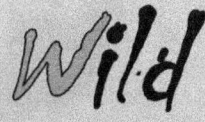

QUOTE

"A poet ought not to pick nature's pocket. Let him borrow, and so borrow as to repay by the very act of borrowing."

Samuel Taylor Coleridge

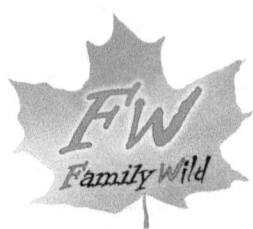

Ok, let's admit it. Sometimes when we are hunting or fishing, prowling after wildflowers or building birdfeeders, cooking wild game or trying to take a picture of a white tailed deer, things can go, well, *wrong*.

And sometimes, that "going wrong" is really, really funny. Maybe not at the time, but eventually, we almost always learn to look back at ourselves and laugh out loud.

I remember a time when my brother took his dog, Burt, on a fishing trip. Now Burt came from bird-dog stock and he always got really, really excited when Brian hooked fish. He'd run up and down the boat, leaping and barking and wagging his tail, sending nets and fishing poles flying.

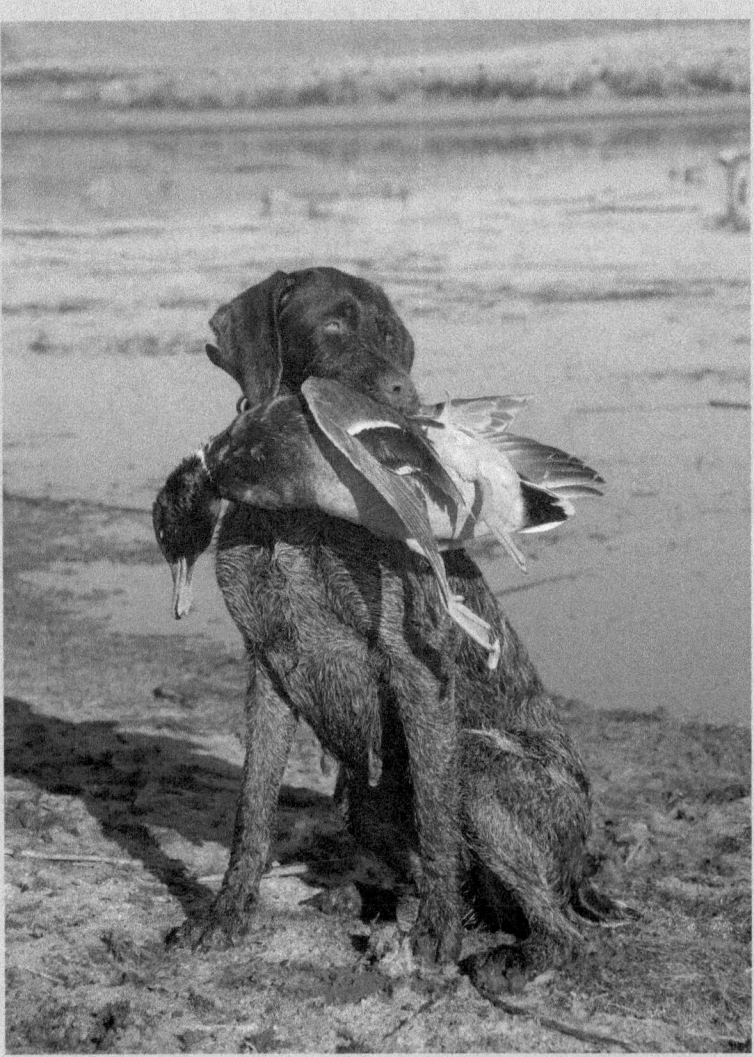

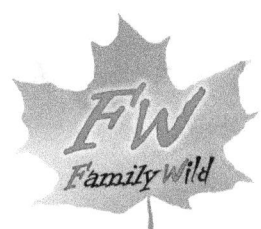

One day, Brian hooked a big northern pike. He pulled it up into the boat with the net, Burt flying around, wild with excitement.

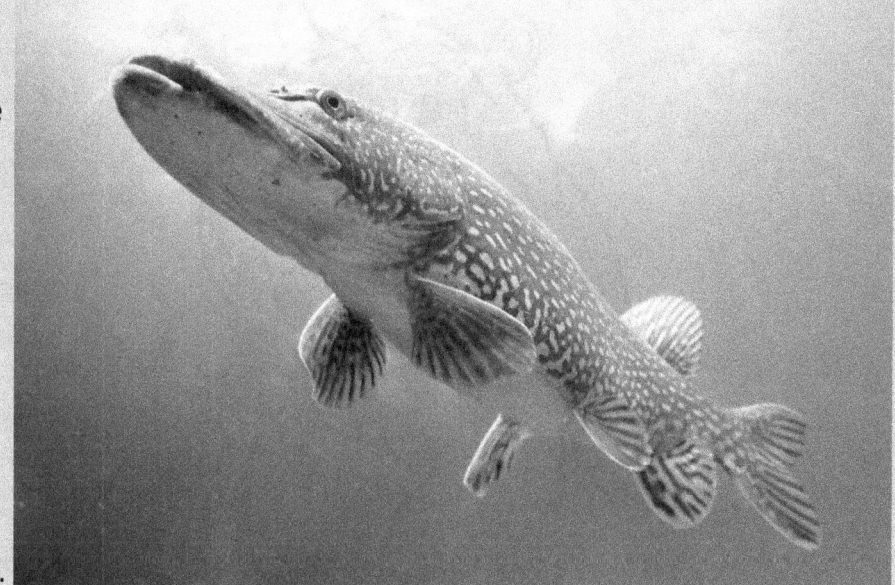

The fish flipped, Burt snapped at him and...ended up attached to the fish. He'd bitten right into the same lure!

Brian reached down, tried to get either the fish or Burt free - and guess what happened? He ended up painfully attached to a fish with a mouthful of teeth, a crazy dog and one nasty treble hooked lure.

Now, I can see you cringing but I bet you are also laughing inside a bit - can you imagine the three of them, fish, man and dog, all trying very hard not to fall overboard? (OK, maybe the fish was hoping for that outcome!) Brian tells this story and people laugh and laugh.

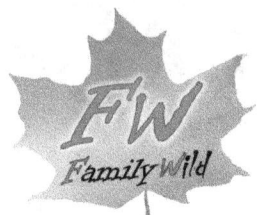

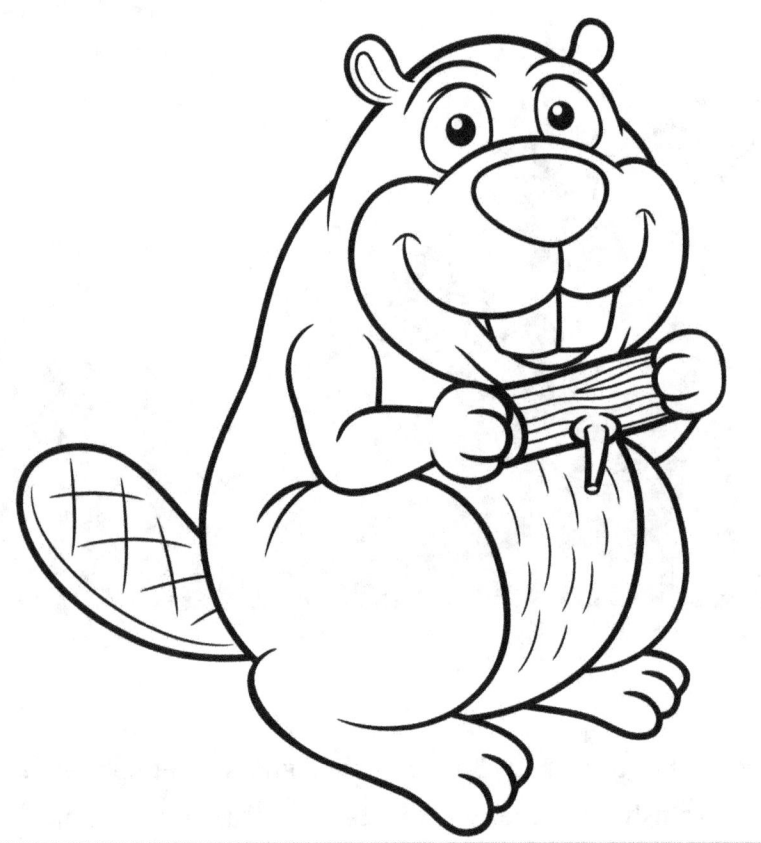

Why? Because crazy stuff does happen in life, we all tend to do something of this sort at some point in our lives and the laughter connects us all. Not any of us is perfect!

So let's take a story like this, one your father or grandmother or friend told, and make it come alive with a comic!

Lots of folks think they can't draw well enough to make a comic come alive, but you'll find lots of internet and book resources on-line and through your local library about drawing comics if you want to work on your skills.

Mostly, it's just a process of breaking down the story and thinking in terms of what kind of picture could show the funny side of what is happening.

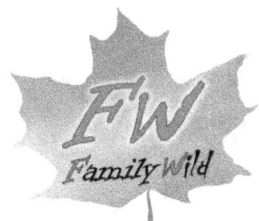

Making your comic strip:

Grab a piece of blank printing paper. Fold your paper in half, then fold it in half again.

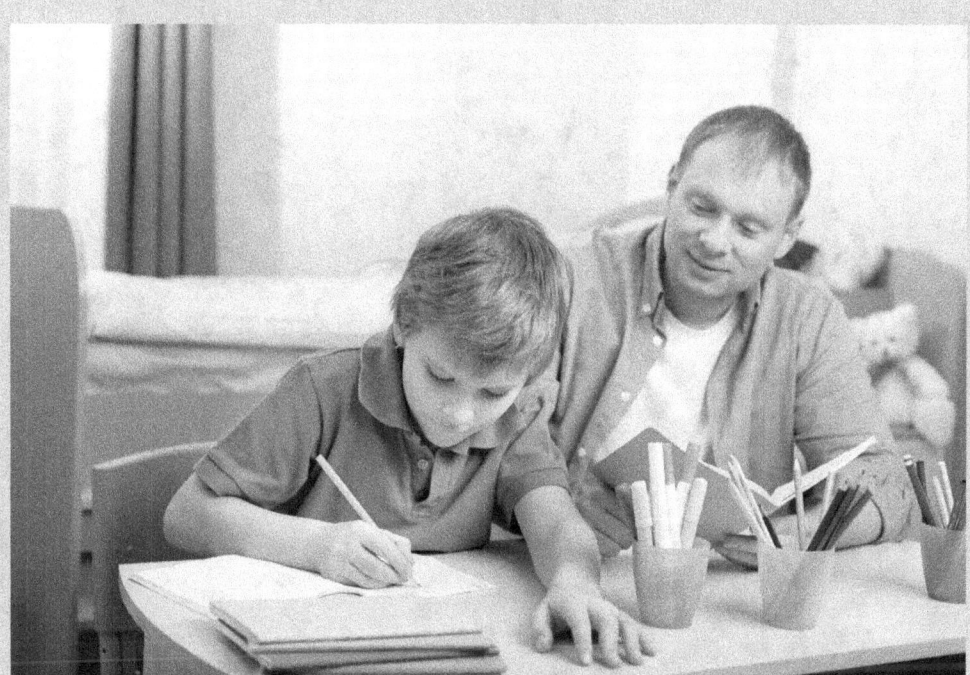

Open it up and using a ruler and ink pen, trace the lines of the folds, creating four boxes on your paper.

Break the story down into four scenes:

The crazy dog on the fishing boat - Brian trying to land a fish

Dog bites fish and gets hooked

Brian gets hooked

Idea bubble over the fish: "Now if I can just get us all back in the water..." or try to find the "funny" part of this episode!

With a pencil, sketch out the scene, one box at a time. You can have your characters speak using idea or word bubbles or you can just put a caption at the bottom of each picture.

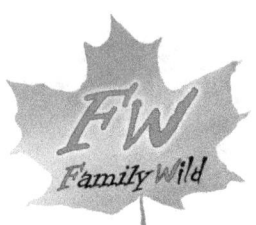

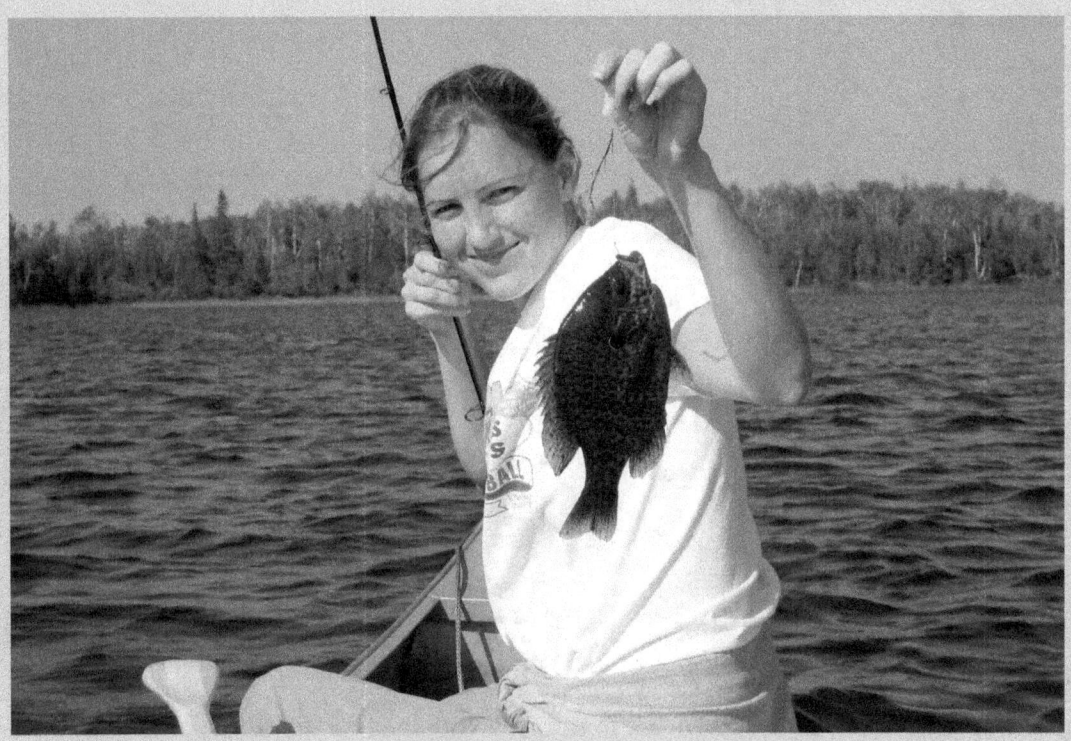

Once you are happy with your pictures and words, use an ink pen to make the comic easier to see and more permanent. It's great to add color, too!

If you have a scanner, capture your comic as a digital image, save it as a jpeg and upload it to your blog Facebook page, add it to your nature journal or keep it with your nature pictures.

Often, we remember the funny times in our lives the best. It's the stuff of great memories, sitting in the fishing camp, laughing about the dog, the fisherman and a really hooked pike. Comics help us find the joy and hilarious in the foibles of our lives, and remind us that we are Wild.

SCRAPBOOK PICTURES

*Glue a couple pictures here
to remember your Activity*

You can keep the pictures in Your Family Wild Activity book,
your own Scrapbook, or put them in a frame
to commemorate your activities years from now!

Below-take a few minutes and tell your ACTIVITY STORY.
In your own words. Think of it as telling the story to
your Grandchildren some day! Do it in your own words
and handwriting-like your sending a post card to
someone 50-100 years from now!

Our Family Wild Activity Story

_____

_____

_____

_____

_____

_____

Family Wild

> "All our dreams can come true, if we have the courage to pursue them."
>
> Walt Disney

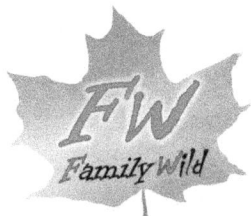
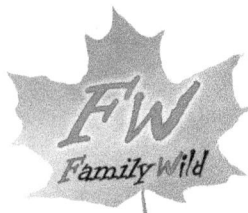

Tanning Hides

NOTE: This process uses battery acid and should not be attempted with very young children present for the tanning portion of the activity. Be very sure you know how to deal with battery acid spills or splashes on you or your clothing. Read on down for this important information.

Objective: utilize the hides of harvested or home-raised animals instead of simply disposing of them

What You Might Need:

FRESH hide (not over an hour old)

Hide Scraper or back of a heavy knife

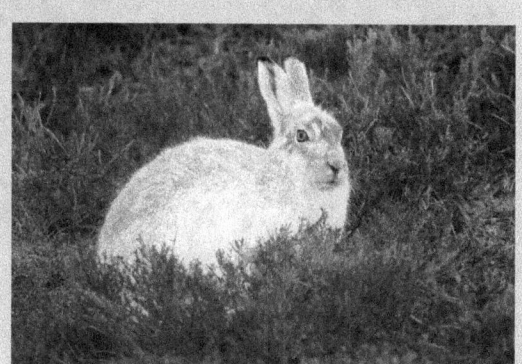

- 7 gallons water
- 16 cups plain salt
- 2 pounds bran flakes
- 3½ cups battery acid (from auto parts store)
- 2 large <u>plastic</u> trashcans and one lid (30-gallon size)
- 2 boxes baking soda
- Neat's-foot oil
- Sponge or paintbrush
- Wood rack or stretcher (wooden pallets will work)
- 4-foot stirring stick (<u>wooden</u>)
- Nails or tacks
- Bristle brush (preferably wire)
- Two big soup pot (for soaking the bran flakes and boiling hot water)
- Strainer or colander
- Rubber gloves, protective eyewear and old clothes

Jump in!

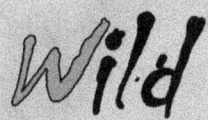

QUOTE

"Fishing provides that connection with the whole living world. It gives you the opportunity of being totally immersed, turning back into yourself in a good way. A form of meditation, some form of communion with levels of yourself that are deeper than the ordinary self."

Ted Hughes

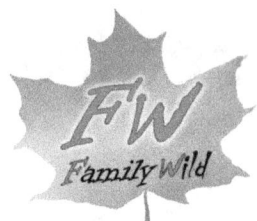

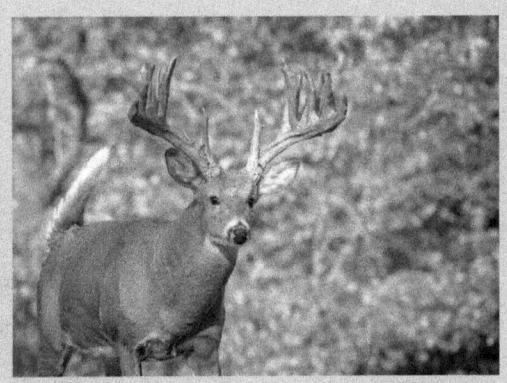

Whether you are harvesting animals in the wild or raising rabbits, sheep, and goats as part of a mini-farm, you will have access to another product that can be enjoyed by the family: the hides! Most tanners charge as much as $60 per raw hide, but you can actually do the work yourself and save a great deal of money. Parts of the process are a little time - consuming and require patience, and like any art you'll become better at it with time. So here we go!

Removing the fat and muscle, salting and drying the skin:

Remove the skin from the animal and scrape off all the fat and muscle tissue. Be careful not to cut through the hide. Then allow the skin to cool. It's best to lay it in a shady place. Lay the hide skin down on a hard surface (think concrete or rock). Once the skin is cool to the touch, COVER the skin with salt. Use a lot-err on the side over doing it. This is what keeps the skin from decomposing.

Allow the skin to completely dry-keep adding salt to areas where moisture pools. Understand it may take a long time for a hide to dry - days to even more than a week. Be sure you are allowing the skin to dry in an area where other animals will not chew or disturb it. When the skin is completely dry to the touch (sort of crispy-feeling), you are all set for the next step.

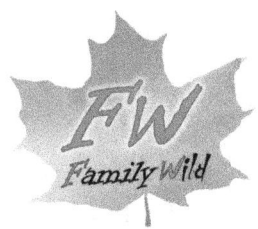

Tanning Method

Be sure you have all the elements listed in the materials list at the beginning of this chapter.

You will need to soak the dried skins in plain, fresh water for two hours prior to tanning to make them flexible. Give them a stir now and then to be sure the hides are fully wetted. Boil three gallons of water in the large soup container and add the bran flakes. Allow to sit for one hour. Strain the bran flakes with the colander or wire strainer and reserve the brown water from the flakes.

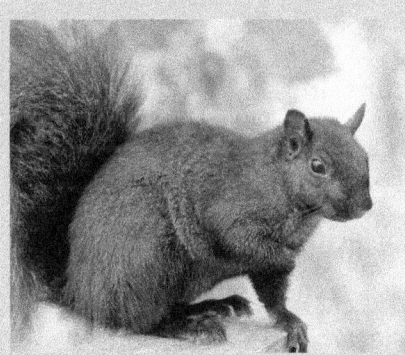

Using the other big soup caldron, boil the remaining four gallons of water.

Pour the boiling water into a trashcan when it is ready.

Add sixteen cups of plain salt to the boiling water in the trash can and stir with the wooden stick until the grains of salt are completely dissolved.

Next, add the bran flake water and stir again until the salt water is wholly mixed with the brownish bran flake water. Allow this trashcan mixture to cool down to a lukewarm temperature.

Next, put on rubber gloves, protective eye-wear and old clothes. Familiarize yourself with how to deal with battery acid spills or acid on yourself. Have your emergency kit at hand. Very carefully, add the battery acid to the water mixture in the trashcan.

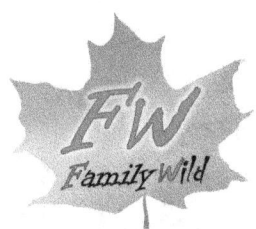

Now you need to peel the inner skin off of your dried hides. If they are truly dry, this should happen fairly easily. When you are done, add them to the battery acid and water mixture. Be very careful not to splash yourself with the acid mixture. **Push the skins under the mixture with the stirring stick and leave them for forty minutes.**

While the hides are soaking, fill another trashcan with fresh, clear water that is lukewarm. Transfer the skins from the battery acid mixture to the clear water **using the wooden stick**. Stir the water with the wooden stick continually. It's hard work, but worth the effort. After about five minutes, change the water.

Do you or your family plan to use the hides close to your skin?

Then you will want to add the baking soda to the water. This actually neutralizes the acid which means you lessen the chance of an allergic reaction but it is also negating the preserving effects of the battery acid. If you are just using the hides on the floor or walls, you can skip adding the baking soda. Use the wooden stick to remove the hides from the rinse water.

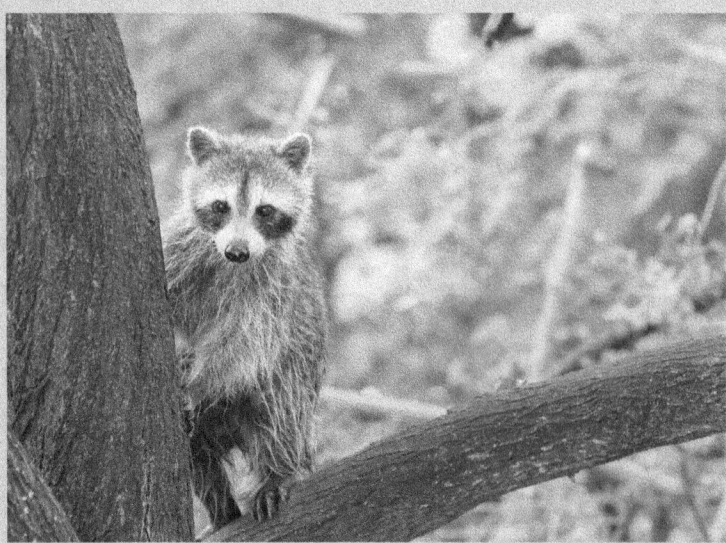

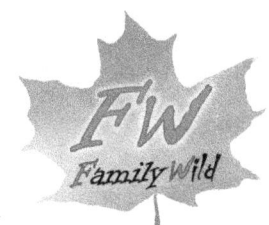

Hang the hides over something sturdy so they can drain fully.

Once the hides are simply damp, use a sponge or paintbrush to apply a layer of neat's-foot oil to the skin side of the hide. Do this very lightly.

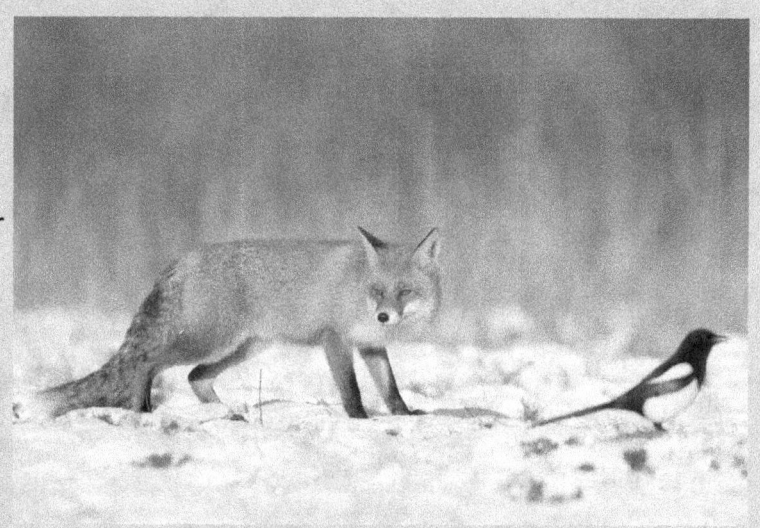

Tack the hide to a wooden stretcher. You can use wood pallets that you salvage from many businesses or create your own frame with found or Restore wood. To tack the hide, use nails or thumb tacks.

Pull the hide very gently as you tack it to the wood. You want it to be taut, but you don't need to strain. Be sure not to rip the hide. Place out of the sun to dry-be sure it is safe from your family dog or any other animal that might enjoy chewing on the hide.

Disposing of your tanning solution:

You can now dispose of your tanning solution; however, you have to do this safely. When you add baking soda to the acid, you'll get a whole lot of bubbling, and a **toxic gas** will be released.

Be sure you have plenty of ventilation and GET AWAY FROM THE GARBAGE CAN UNTIL THE PROCESS IS COMPLETE. The baking soda neutralizes the acid-err on the side of too much baking soda.

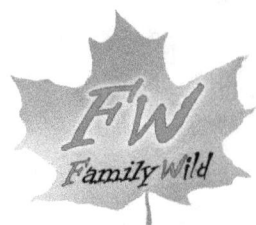

DO NOT POUR THIS DOWN THE DRAIN. It can be used to kill weeds - some folks use it on their gravel driveways to keep down green growth. Also, dispose of it far away from your well.

Checking on Your Hide:

During the drying period, you need to check your hide every day. Very dry areas can be gently touched up with the Neatsfoot oil. You can take the hide off the wooden rack when it feels dry in the center. It will be flexible and soft.

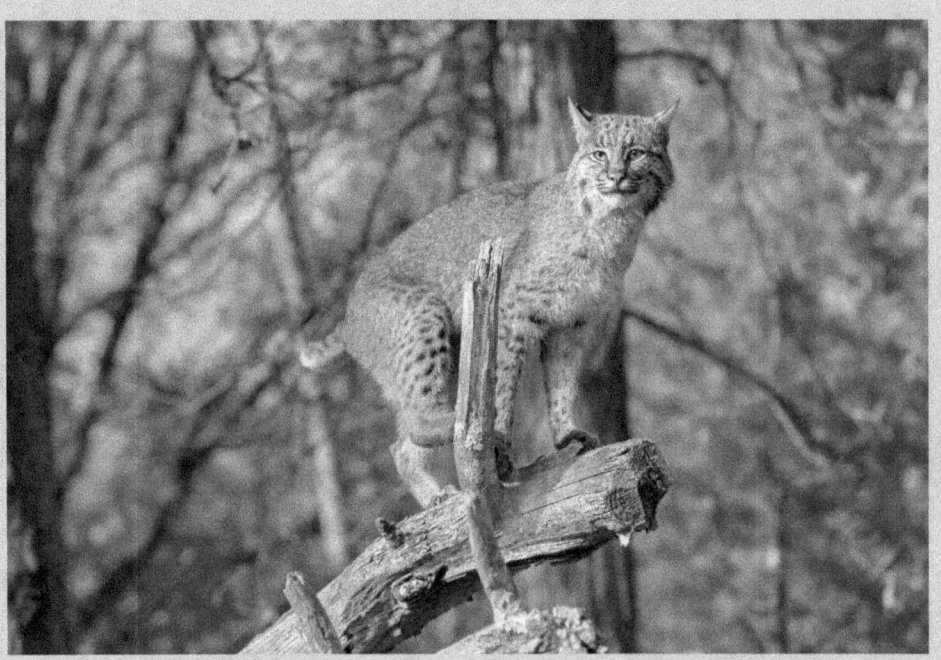

Use the wire brush on the skin side of the hide to rough it slightly and lighten the color. Be very careful and gentle so you do not damage your project.

Allow the hide to dry completely for a few more days and you are ready to put it to use!

And that is the Wild way to use all of the animals you harvest!

SCRAPBOOK PICTURES

*Glue a couple pictures here
to remember your Activity*

You can keep the pictures in Your Family Wild Activity book,
your own Scrapbook, or put them in a frame
to commemorate your activities years from now!

Below-take a few minutes and tell your ACTIVITY STORY.
In your own words. Think of it as telling the story to
your Grandchildren some day! Do it in your own words
and handwriting-like your sending a post card to
someone 50-100 years from now!

Our Family Wild Activity Story

_____

_____

_____

_____

_____

_____

Family Wild

> "How wonderful it is that nobody need wait a single moment before beginning to improve the world."
>
> Anne Frank

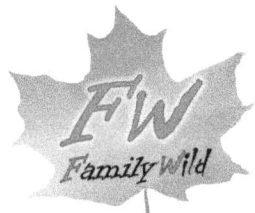
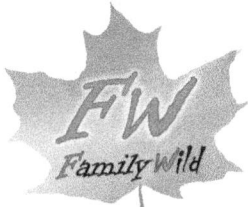

Wildlife Taxidermy

Objective: create a set of questions to ask a professional taxidermist. Visit a shop and find out how he or she got started.

What You Might Need:

Appointment with an area taxidermist - ask for just fifteen minutes of their time

Paper and pen

Camera or smart phone
List of questions

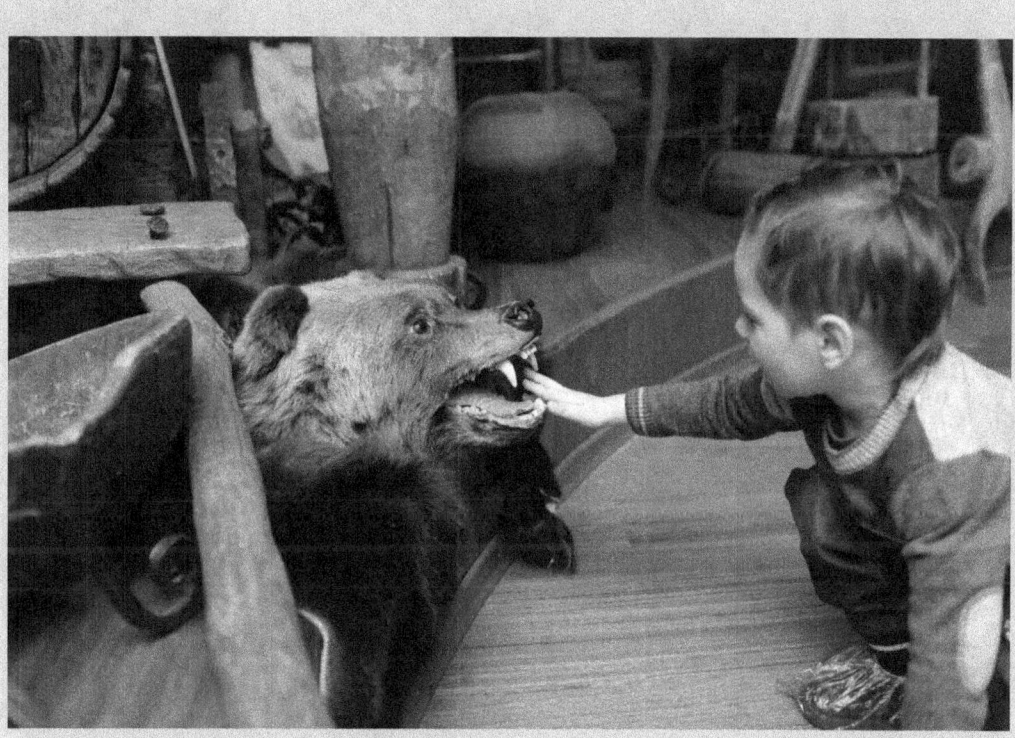

Jump in!

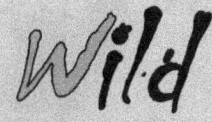 **QUOTE**

"What the caterpillar calls the end of the world the master calls a butterfly."
Richard Bach

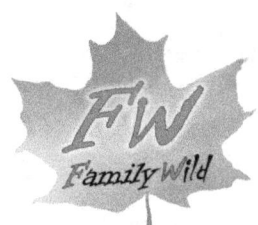

Sometimes when a hunter or fisherman (woman) ends up with a really nice animal, they want to preserve the way the creature looked in the wild.

Way back when people painted on caves, it was animals they most sketched - the source of their food and the amazing other beings they shared their world with.

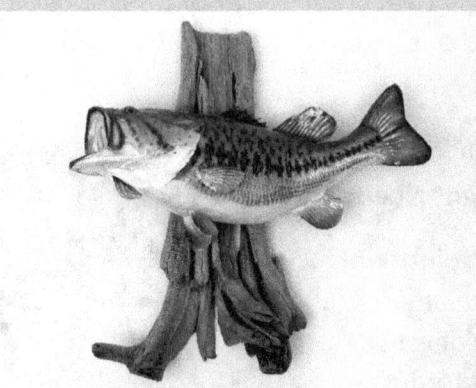

We hang wildlife art in our homes, send wildlife cards to folks at Christmas, wear wildlife sweatshirts or necklaces. Animals and fish are beautiful - their fur or scales or feathers are full of life and color and textures, and it is quite normal to want to capture that somehow, to bring it home and appreciate the creature in a way that is realistic and almost "alive".

A taxidermist is someone who knows how to preserve hides and create frames that make the pelts come to life again. But usually, you don't open up a college course book and find taxidermy 101.

How did these folks get started with their art? What's all involved, moving from a fresh deer head to a mounted and preserved specimen? Well, it's time to get Wild and go ask!

First, identify the different taxidermists in your area. Ask them if there might be a good time to stop by their shop and ask them a few questions (this could, by the way, be just the thing for your personal blog, journal or newspaper article...or maybe you'll get a good comic strip idea out of the visit!)

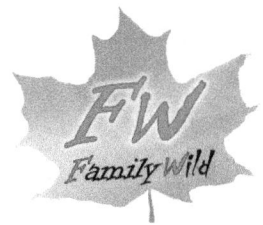

Next, take the time to write down a few questions. Sometimes when we meet someone, we are shy or they are shy and that's hard to get the conversation going. So go in with your questions in hand - and ask what you really want to know!

For example, how did this taxidermist learn to do his or her art? Does anyone else in his or her family do this? What was the hardest part to learn? Are there parts of it the taxidermist doesn't like to do? What tools does he or she

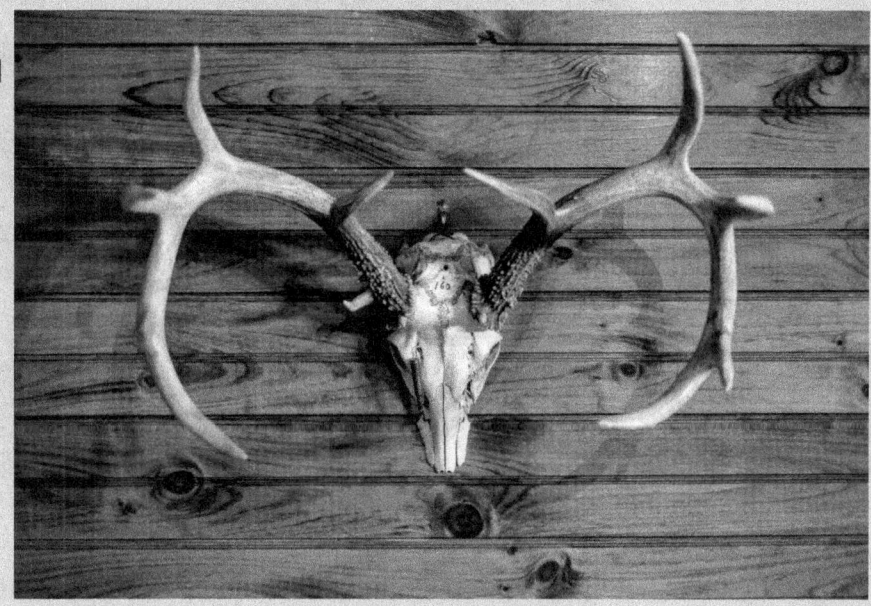

use? Does he or she compete in art shows? How do you learn more if you are interested in this sort of hobby or work?

Then, keep your appointment! If the weather turns bad or you get sick or the car won't start, be sure to check in and let the taxidermist know you can't make it that day. Try to set up another day! This will make him or her remember and trust you - that you cared enough to be interested and were concerned you couldn't make it.

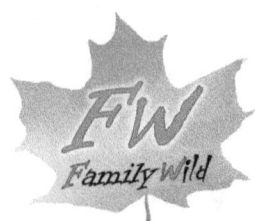

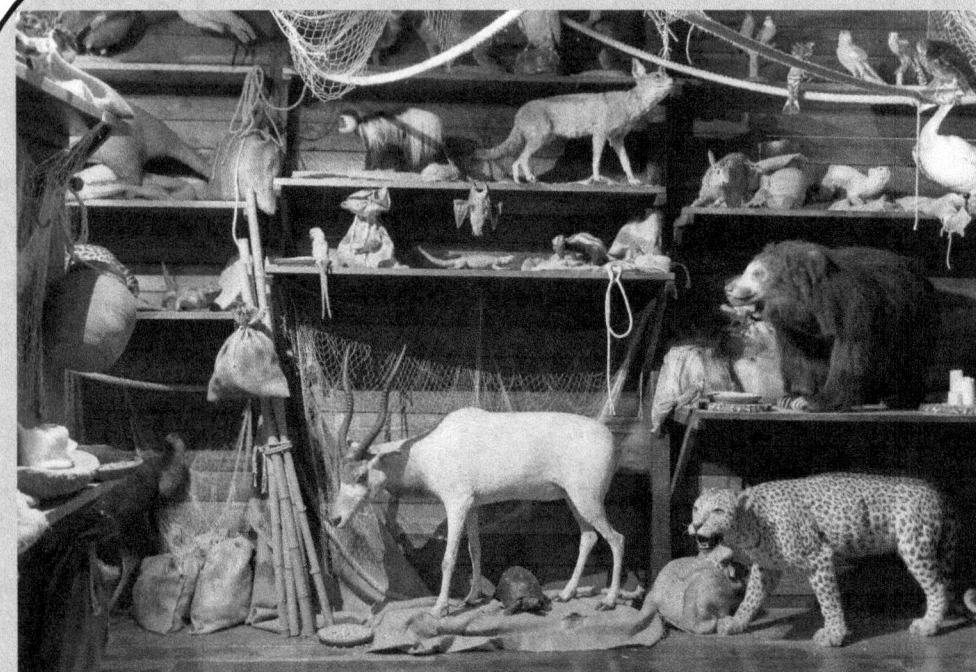

When you meet with the taxidermist, write down the answers to your questions if you want, or maybe even record the session with your smartphone. Take a few pictures if it is OK with the shop owner. It's really nice if you say thank you at the end of your conversation and even better if you send him or her a little thank-you card or letter.

Keep your questions and answer in your nature journal. You can refer to them later and use them in lots of different ways for school writing projects or other activities in this book! Be sure to write down what you learned, what interested you, what really made you go "ick", if you liked the mounted animals or not - this is you space to explore and be honest!

There are many jobs and hobbies that work with nature - this is the first step to exploring all those Wild ideas.

SCRAPBOOK PICTURES

*Glue a couple pictures here
to remember your Activity*

You can keep the pictures in Your Family Wild Activity book,
your own Scrapbook, or put them in a frame
to commemorate your activities years from now!

Below-take a few minutes and tell your ACTIVITY STORY.
In your own words. Think of it as telling the story to
your Grandchildren some day! Do it in your own words
and handwriting-like your sending a post card to
someone 50-100 years from now!

Our Family Wild Activity Story

_____

_____

_____

_____

_____

_____

Family Wild

> You see things; and you say "Why?" But I dream things that never were; and I say "Why not?"
>
> George Bernard Shaw

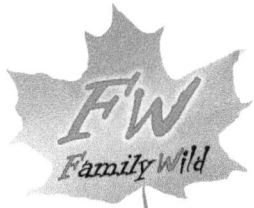 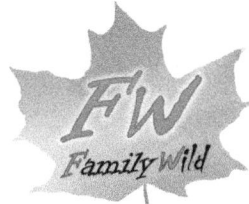

Capturing Animal Tracks

Objective: Create a collection of animal tracks using plaster, identify animals, keep track of dates when the tracks were found.

What You Might Need:

Plaster of Paris-five to ten lb. bag

Quart-sized zip lock bags

Thermos or two of water

Small plastic dish to measure the plaster and water

Old butter knife or small garden trowel

Back pack

Paper clip

Small notebook and pen

Something to mix plaster with-heavy twig, old plastic spoon, etc.

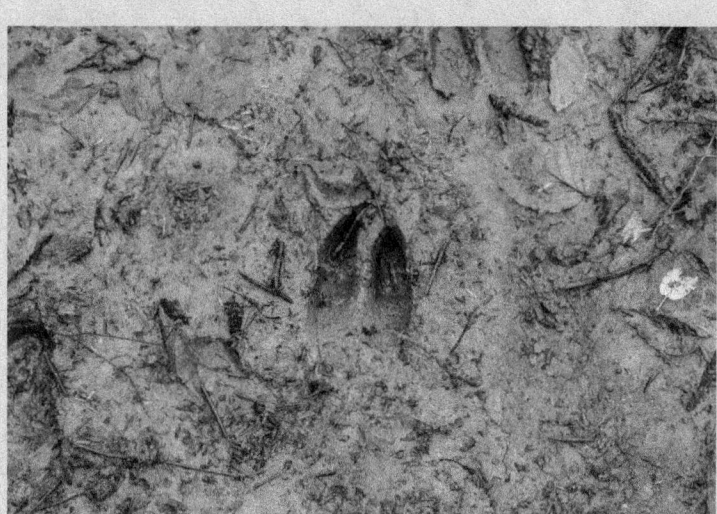

Jump in!

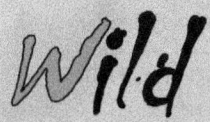

QUOTE

"If I had to describe the scent of Michigan in spring and summer, it wouldn't be a particular smell – blooming wildflowers or boat exhaust off the lake – it would be a color: Green."

Viola Shipman, The Charm Bracelet

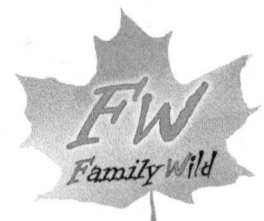

One of the most fun things you can do on your spring, fall or summer-time nature walks is to create Plaster of Paris casts of animal tracks. In a backpack, assemble everything on the list above.

You can put a pre-measured amount of plaster into one quart-sized zip lock bags, making three or four bags to take with you.

Search carefully on your walk. The best tracks are often left in mud along river banks, or along dirt roads after a rainstorm.

Although it is easy to find tracks in snow, the plaster does not set up well in cold temperatures and snow tracks are often too fragile to cast

When you find a clean and deep track, first build a dam around the image-you'll want it about 1 inch high, and can make it out of rocks or loose dirt. Next, take out one of your bags of plaster and mix in the water. If you measured two cups of plaster into your bag, you'll need one cup of water to mix in with it. (Always figure two parts plaster to one part water)

Stir quickly, getting out most of the lumps. It should look a little like pancake batter.

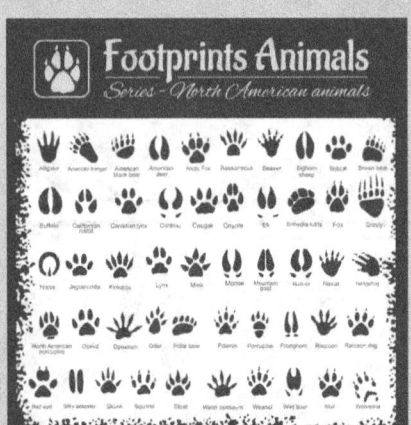

Carefully pour the plaster into the animal track first, the "flood" the dam-area to the edges. Smooth the plaster out, and when it has set a little bit, you can write the date and place where you found the track.

You can also push a paperclip into the plaster, at the top of the cast, so you can hang your image on a wall later. Be sure to leave a rounded tip of the paperclip out of the plaster!!!

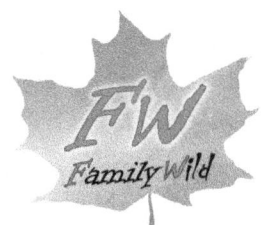

Usually, the cast will set up in about fifteen minutes. During this time, you might Make a note in your notebook as well-how much plaster did you use? Where was the track found? What date? What animal do you think it might be?

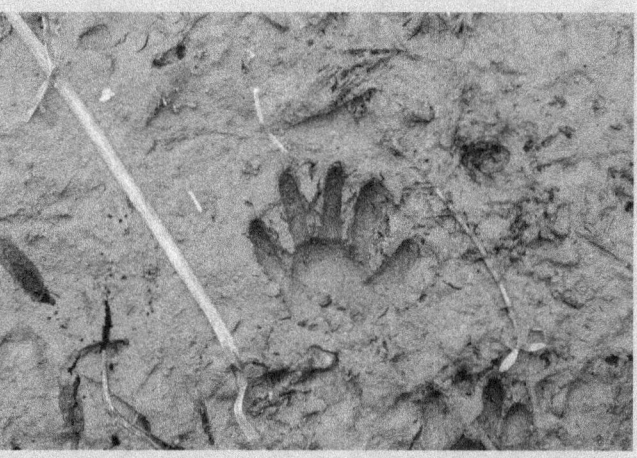

Pull the dam down carefully, exposing the edges of the cast. Does it feel like it has set up enough to move? If not, give it a few more minutes of drying time, then gently remove it from the earth.

Don't worry about all the dirt on the image - you can carefully brush off the loose material after you have let the cast dry in a warm area for a day or two.

At home, after a full day or two of drying time, use a small toothbrush or paper towel to brush off any dirt you don't want. It's nice to leave a little-it creates a contrast for the image.

If you take all the dirt off, you can also lightly go over with white cast with a thin whisper of paint. To do this, choose a brown or deep green acrylic, dip the paint brush lightly, and brush a few times over a paper towel until you see almost no paint. Then brush across the cast. This will leave a light veneer of paint that will pull the image of the print into high relief.

Using a book or internet, try to identify the print, and write the name of animal on the back of the cast. Over time, you can create a wonderful collection of prints-birds, mammals and maybe even reptile images. It's a fun way to bring the Wild home!

SCRAPBOOK PICTURES

Glue a couple pictures here to remember your Activity

You can keep the pictures in Your Family Wild Activity book, your own Scrapbook, or put them in a frame to commemorate your activities years from now!

Below-take a few minutes and tell your ACTIVITY STORY. In your own words. Think of it as telling the story to your Grandchildren some day! Do it in your own words and handwriting-like your sending a post card to someone 50-100 years from now!

Our Family Wild Activity Story

_____

_____

_____

_____

_____

_____

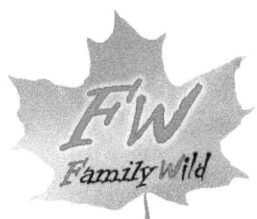
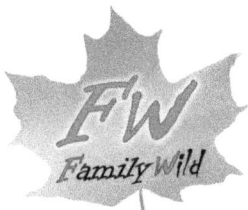

Build a Worm Composter

Objective: Repurposing of plastic containers to create both compost for the garden and fishing bait, while learning the basic life-cycle of worms and our own organic garbage.

What You Might Need:

A large plastic container, such as an old Igloo ice chest (the wheels are great for moving your composter around), or snap-top plastic storage bin

Power drill

Soil

Plant material

Worms *(can be ordered online. Backyard night crawlers will not work!!!)*

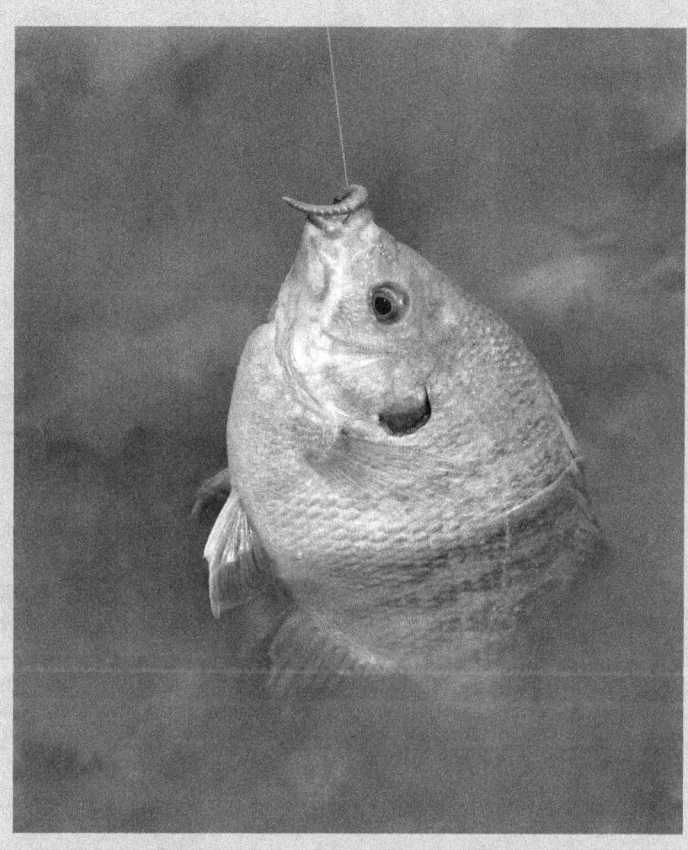

Jump in!

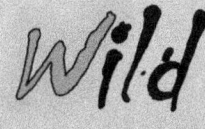

QUOTE

"Some of the best times I've spent in Colorado have been in the backcountry with my mom and siblings, and more recently, with my own kids. That is why I'm concerned to see today's kids spending more time browsing the Internet than exploring nature."

Mark Udall

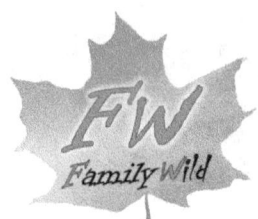

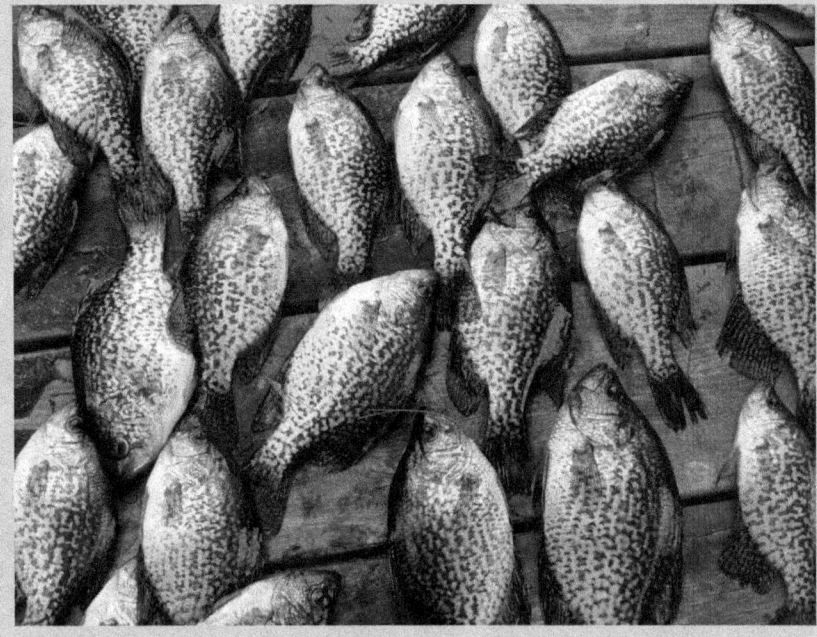

Vermiculture is just a big word that means you raise worms for composting or as bait for fishing. It's pretty easy to create a do-it-yourself worm bin. So here we go.

The worms you want to use are called Red Wigglers or *Eisenia fetida*. These worms can be purchased on-line and are sometimes available locally. Worms eat up to ½ their body weight in a day (but remember that worms themselves are quite small and all you may need to compost all the fresh veggies from your kitchen). If you start with ¼ lb. or so of worms, they certainly will multiply over time.

Using a simple dark-sided plastic tote, drill a bunch of $1/16^{th}$ inch holes in the lid for air to get in. You can also drill tiny holes in the bottom to help with drainage. Some seepage will occur---this liquid is a rich fertilizer known as worm pee! You can place a catch basin under your bin and pour this liquid at the base of your house plants or use in your garden.

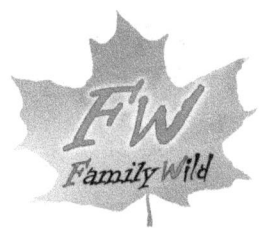

Place a piece of wetted cardboard at the bottom of the worm bin, then fill the bin about half-way with wet newspaper, dirt, and just a little well-aged manure if you have it. Don't add fresh manure - it will heat up and kill your worms. Mix all this together, then add your worms and cover the top. Every few days, add kitchen scraps to the worm composter - it helps to gently work the scraps into the soil.

Use a spray bottle to spritz the newspaper bed with water if it seems to be drying out a lot; you may need to periodically add more damp shredded newspapers as the old ones decompose and get eaten. Some worm-raisers have noted that If your worms are crawling up the sides of your bin, it may be too wet inside.

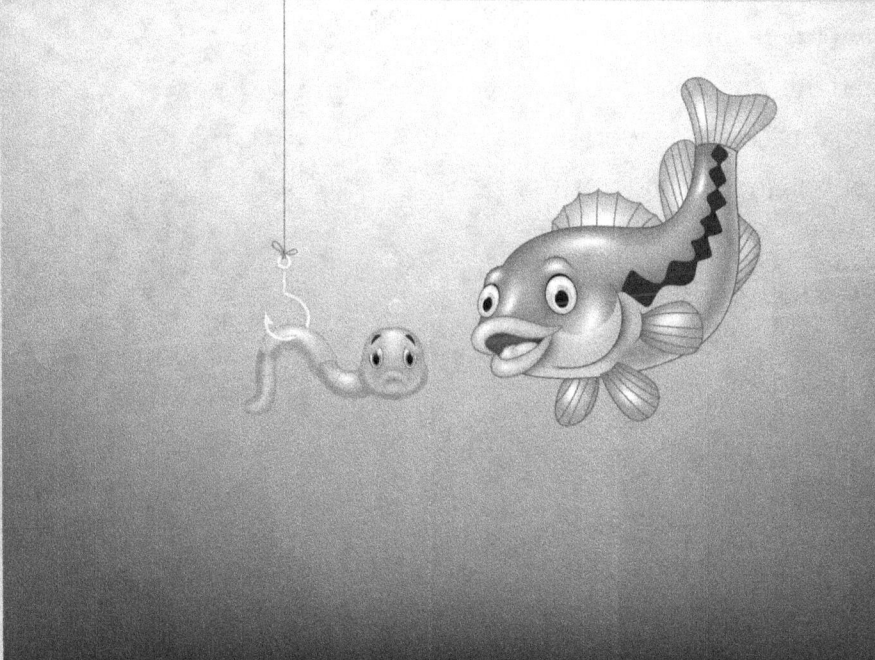

Keep your bin in a cool place. Worms prefer temperatures between 40-80 degrees Fahrenheit. They like it cool and dark and damp. Worms don't do well in your outside compost bin because those composters heat up much higher than this and that kills them dead.

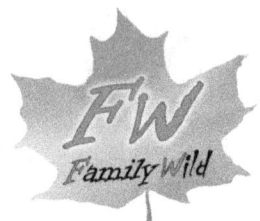

Be careful what you feed - no dairy, crush up egg fresh egg shells, no dog or cat poop, limit the amount of skins of oranges, lemons and grapefruit, no meat products.

To use the castings (worm poop), it is easiest to set up a station and gently take out a hand full of dirt and spread out on some newspaper. Pick the worms out or bunch up some fresh dirt-they will move toward it and you can scrape the casting into a bucket for use in your garden.

Explore the internet using sources on our blog - there are some great websites and YouTube programs about vermiculture you may want to check out.

That's the way to get Wild with your fertilizer!

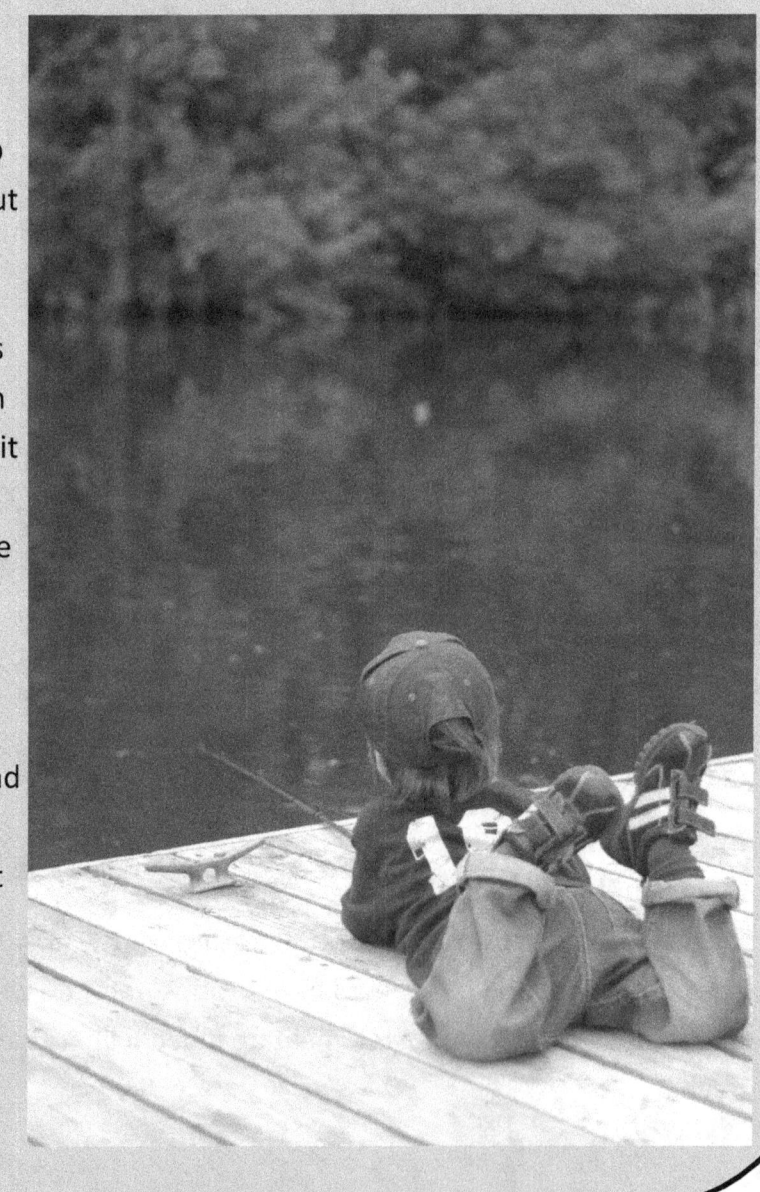

SCRAPBOOK PICTURES

Glue a couple pictures here
to remember your Activity

You can keep the pictures in Your Family Wild Activity book, your own Scrapbook, or put them in a frame to commemorate your activities years from now!

Below-take a few minutes and tell your ACTIVITY STORY. In your own words. Think of it as telling the story to your Grandchildren some day! Do it in your own words and handwriting-like your sending a post card to someone 50-100 years from now!

Our Family Wild Activity Story

_____

_____

_____

_____

_____

_____

_____

Family Wild

> "What we are is God's gift to us. What we become is our gift to God."
>
> Eleanor Powell

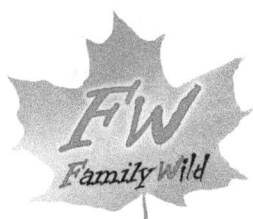
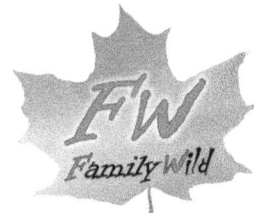

Hatch Butterflies

Objective: identify a Monarch caterpillar and milkweed plants. Care for the caterpillar, observe the changes from small larvae to chrysalis to mature butterfly. Learn about Monarch migration and lifecycles.

What you might need:

Identify Milkweed in your area or plant milkweed seeds

Image of a Monarch caterpillar

Quart-sized canning jar

Canning lid

Nail and hammer

Camera or smartphone

Journal and pen

Butterfly book or access to internet

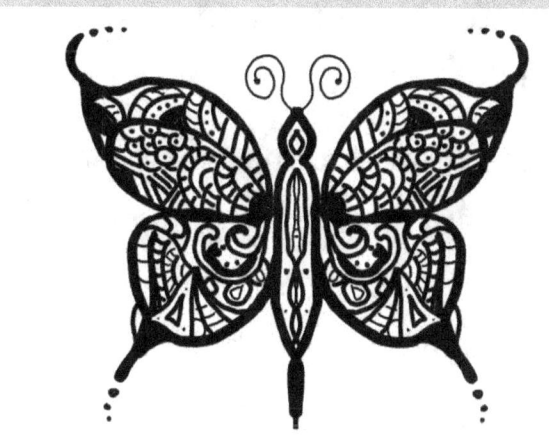

Jump In!

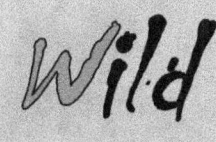

QUOTE

"The violets in the mountains have broken the rocks."

Author - Tennessee Williams

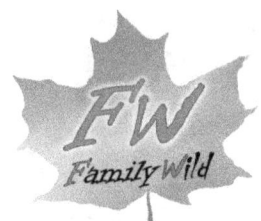

One of the most amazing activities you can do is watch a tiny striped caterpillar grow big and fat and then hang themselves in a chrysalis and transform into a butterfly. It's fun and easy, too.

First, create your habitat. Find a big jar with a tight-fitting lid. You'll need to use the hammer and a nail to punch holes in the lid-all animals need air to live! Next, using a book about local plants or the internet,

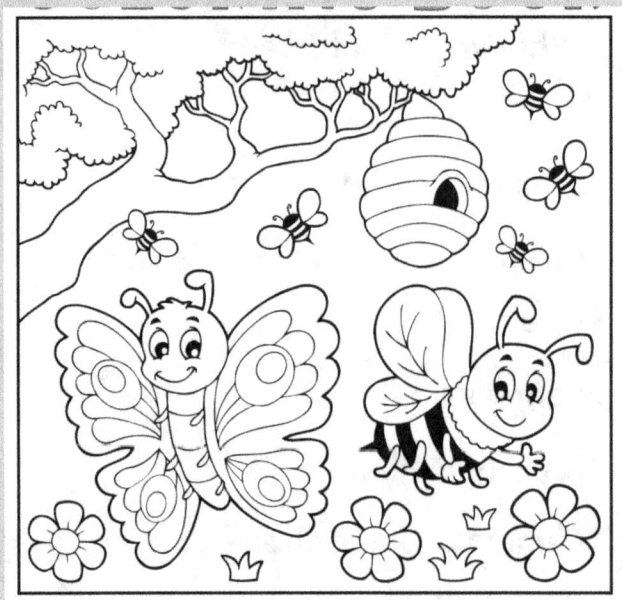

identify what Milkweed looks like. Take nature walks, looking for this plant.

Can't find any in your area? Then consider growing some right in your own garden. These butterflies are very specific about what they eat-and their habitat has been growing smaller over the years. If you are lucky, the caterpillar's will appear right in your own garden. Be patient -sometimes it takes time for the adult Monarchs to find your patch!

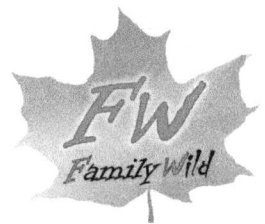

Once you have found the right plant, bring your jar with you and start looking at the leaves-the caterpillars chew in a kind of half-moon pattern. If you see this, gently lift the leaves. Once you find the caterpillar (refer to your butterfly book from the library or an image you found on the internet).

With great care, transfer the caterpillar to your jar and pluck a few leaves for him to eat. Put the lid on the jar and take the small creature right home.

Place it in an area that won't get in the sunlight, and that won't be jostled by anyone. Add new fresh leaves every day, and keep track of how fast the caterpillar grows by taking a picture of it and dating the photo. This can be added to your nature journal!

At some point, the little guy will spin a fine web and hang himself in a J-shape from the top of the jar. At this point, it's very important not to remove the lid or shake the jar in any way.

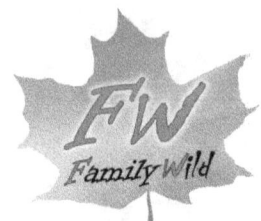

In very little time, you will see him make the chrysalis, and the transformation into the butterfly has begun. Take pictures every day, and notice the changes in the color of the chrysalis...soon you will see it begin to change from a light green to the color of a monarch.

If you happen to catch the time when the butterfly begins to emerge, don't try to help it out!!!! Just watch...the little butterfly will crawl out and clinging to the now-clear chrysalis wall, it will begin to beat its wings, sending fluid out to help it bloom and take on its final shape.

It's OK to carefully take the top off the jar, and using your little finger, get the butterfly to cling to you. Take it outside and very carefully encourage it to step onto a branch or part of plant in your garden.

Keep taking pictures! Eventually, the butterfly will fill out its wings and flutter away. Be sure to put the date and time and where you released the Monarch in your nature journal. You have just helped one species continue to create beauty in our world. And that is Wild.

SCRAPBOOK PICTURES

*Glue a couple pictures here
to remember your Activity*

You can keep the pictures in Your Family Wild Activity book,
your own Scrapbook, or put them in a frame
to commemorate your activities years from now!

Below-take a few minutes and tell your ACTIVITY STORY.
In your own words. Think of it as telling the story to
your Grandchildren some day! Do it in your own words
and handwriting-like your sending a post card to
someone 50-100 years from now!

Our Family Wild Activity Story

_____

_____

_____

_____

_____

_____

Family Wild

> "If not us, who?
>
> If not now, when?"
>
> Hillel the Elder

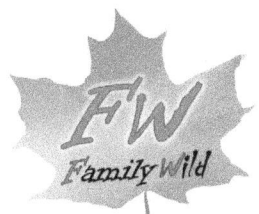
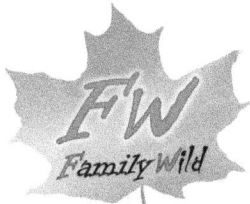

Make Your Own Fish Scaler

Objective: Repurpose materials to create a pan-fish scaler.

What You Might Need:

A wooden handle of some kind from an old hammer for instance, or a de-barked handle-sized chunk of very hard wood

Nails

Hammer

Bottle cap with rough edges

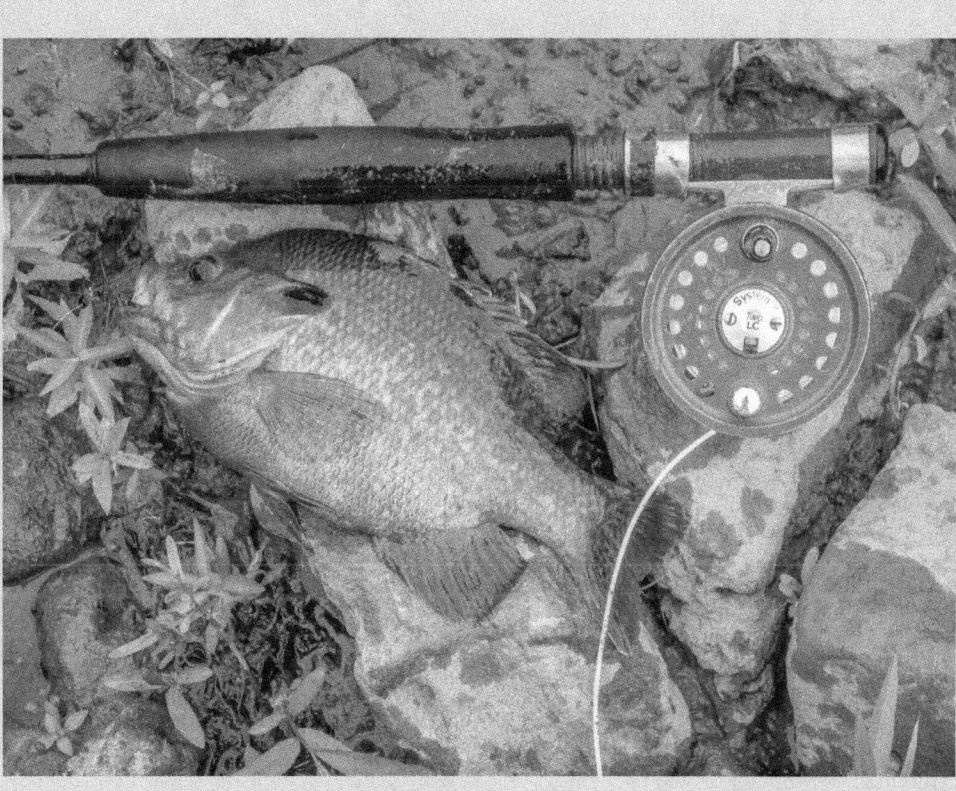

Jump in!

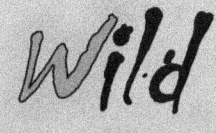

QUOTE

"The more often we see the things around us - even the beautiful and wonderful things - the more they become invisible to us. That is why we often take for granted the beauty of this world: the flowers, the trees, the birds, the clouds - even those we love. Because we see things so often, we see them less and less."

Joseph B. Wirthlin

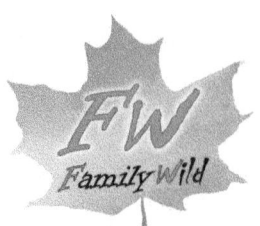

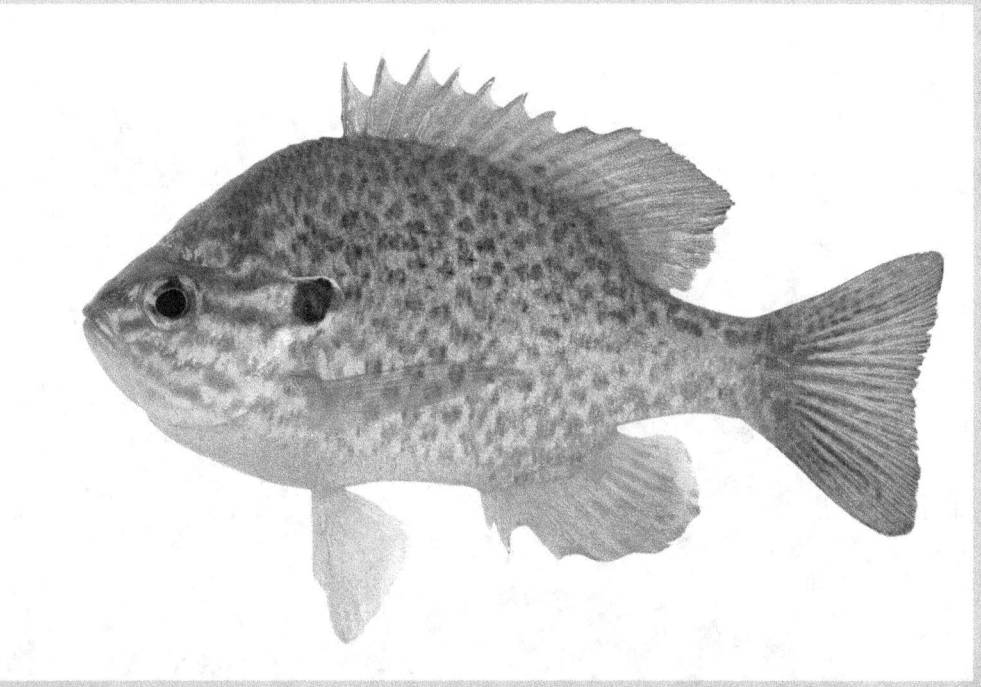

Pan fish (think perch or bluegills or sunfish) are lovely to fry up with their skins intact - except those scales have to GO! This project is a neat way to make a compact and effective fish scaler from "found" objects that my father learned from his father---and now it's handed down to you!

If you are looking for a suitable handle, be sure to stop by a resale store, root through your grandfather's old barn or even post what you need on internet giveaway sites. You may be able to find one in your woodpile, too!

Same with the bottle caps-ask around if you don't have any "rough edged" bottle caps. They are getting harder to find. You might try a restaurant or two-perhaps they are just throwing them away and would love to "rehome" them for your project if it gets more stuff out of their trash!

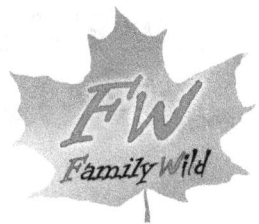

To make the scaler, simply nail the back of the bottle cap to the piece of wood or old handle! You can paint the handle if you wish or wrap it with textured tape to make it easier to grip.

To use the scaler, simple hold the fish up at its head and rub the rough edge of the bottle cap AGAINST the way the scales hug the fish.

You have to be pretty rough when you do this. Once the fish is all scaled, rinse it off and then go ahead and fillet as usual, leaving the skin intact.

Pretty Wild way to make use of old junk, huh?

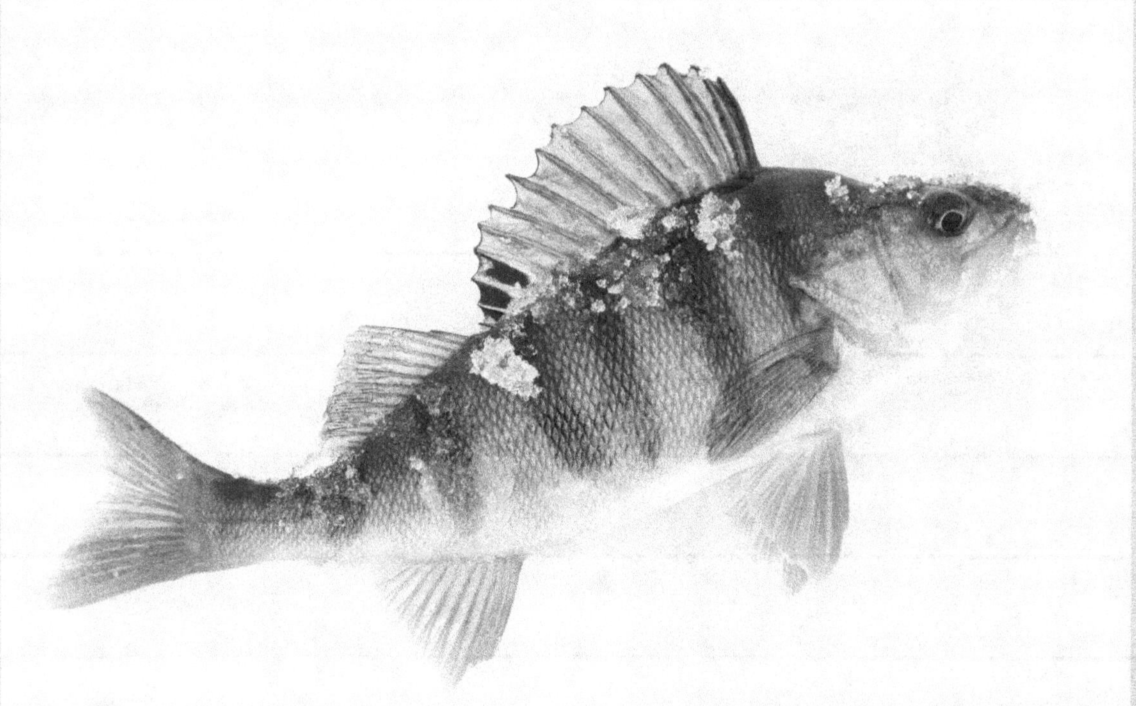

SCRAPBOOK PICTURES

*Glue a couple pictures here
to remember your Activity*

You can keep the pictures in Your Family Wild Activity book,
your own Scrapbook, or put them in a frame
to commemorate your activities years from now!

Below-take a few minutes and tell your ACTIVITY STORY.
In your own words. Think of it as telling the story to
your Grandchildren some day! Do it in your own words
and handwriting-like your sending a post card to
someone 50-100 years from now!

Our Family Wild Activity Story

_____

_____

_____

_____

_____

_____

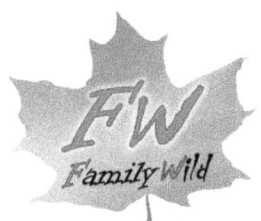
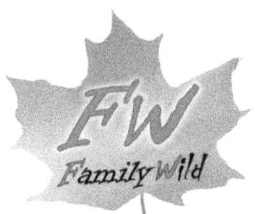

Night Crawler Ninja

Objective: learn to pick your own bait right out of your back yard.

What You Might Need:

A container that will not allow light in, punctured with small air holes on the top and sides

Damp newspaper

Flashlight

Quiet shoes

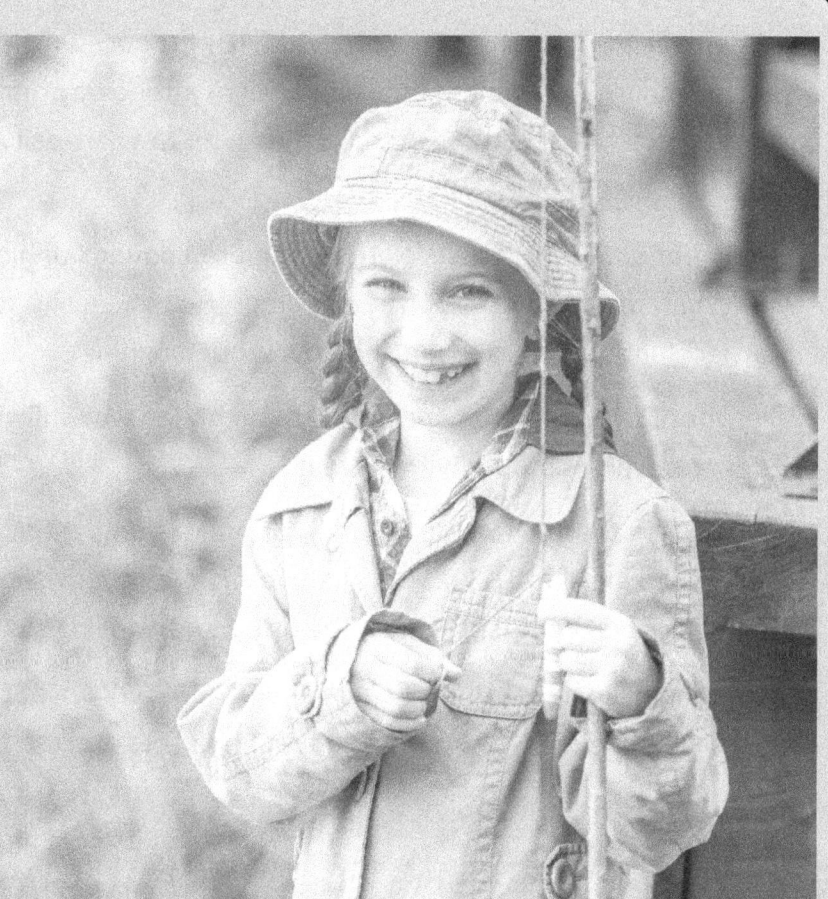

Jump in!

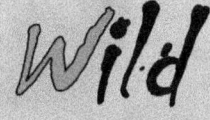

QUOTE

"One must ask children and birds how cherries and strawberries taste."

Johann Wolfgang von Goethe

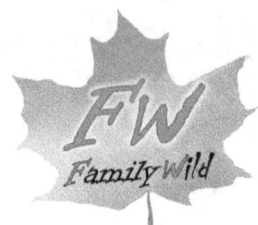

I remember the first time my husband Mike introduced night-crawler hunting to our son and me. We waited until a cool night after a day of rain in the summer. Lights turned off in the house, and armed with the bait-pail and flashlight, Ian and I stood waiting.

Mike crept out of the house, all three hundred pounds of him stepping delicately, lightly, with poised and alert freeze-frames. He looked like some kind of Night-Crawler Hunting Ninja and Ian and I burst out laughing.

Like worms are gonna run and hide, I thought. Ian was still giggling, but at least trying to cover his mouth with his hands.

Mike flashed the light on the ground, careful to shine at the edges of where he was actually looking, and THERE! Our first worm. It lay over the earth, one end of it disappearing down its small hole, the other end, moving slowly side to side.

Mike tiptoed up, crooked his fingers and STABBED down at the little worm, capturing it between his thumb and first finger. He exerted the tiniest, steadiest

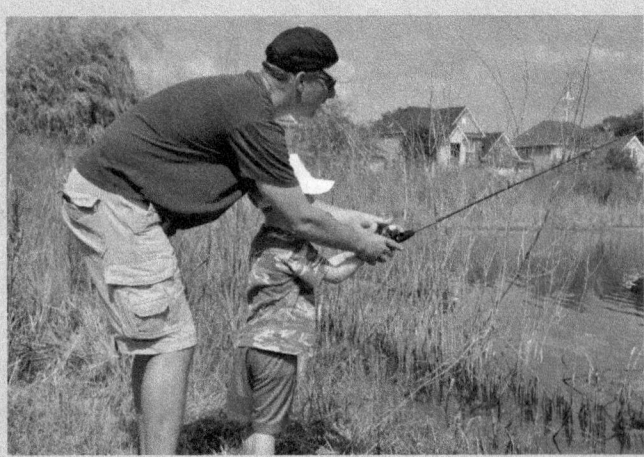

pressure. Finally, the worm slid free of its hole and the Night-crawler Ninja held it up proudly.

Ian and I looked at him and howled.

He immediately placed the worm in the bucket and without a word, motioned for us to try.

So we did.

We stopped laughing pretty quickly.

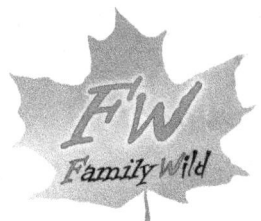

Night-crawlers are wicked-fast! No kidding! The one I was aiming for felt my step or sensed the way the light was falling on him and faster than you can blink, he sucked himself back down his little hole and disappeared. I stood up, fingers still ready for the grab and totally skunked.

Now Mike was laughing. Hard.

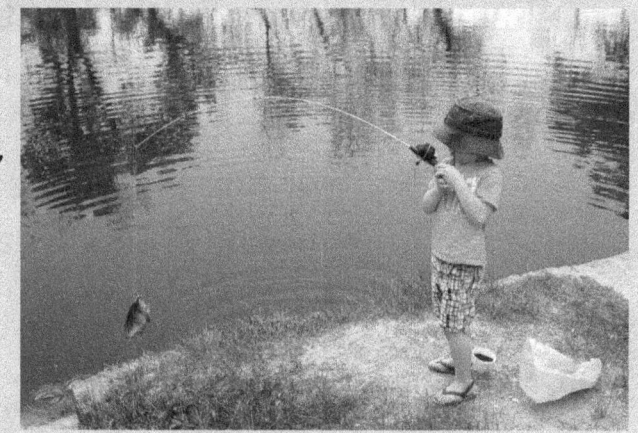

It took a while to learn to step softly, to keep the light off the shiny little bodies, to make quick and decisive grabs but not pull so hard once you had the worm that it broke in two. (Never put a half a worm in a container-it will actually kill the rest of your harvest.)

So find yourself a container. Put a little damp newspaper or paper towels in to keep the worms moist. Arm yourself with a flashlight and get ready to be a Night Crawler Ninja. You may find a red-colored light works better if you have one. Feel free to try different colors. You can use colored plastic see-through materials to try different light.

There is still no better fish bait than a fat juicy worm. (Have your parents price a dozen night crawlers at a local bait shop-you'll be surprised how much money your family will save if you fish with them!) When you are done for the evening, put the container in your refrigerator.

Oh, and if you don't use the worms in a few weeks, be sure to throw the container out. No, don't open it...there is not a worse smell in all the world! You don't want to be *too* Wild near your family's refrigerator!

SCRAPBOOK PICTURES

*Glue a couple pictures here
to remember your Activity*

You can keep the pictures in Your Family Wild Activity book,
your own Scrapbook, or put them in a frame
to commemorate your activities years from now!

Below-take a few minutes and tell your ACTIVITY STORY.
In your own words. Think of it as telling the story to
your Grandchildren some day! Do it in your own words
and handwriting-like your sending a post card to
someone 50-100 years from now!

Our Family Wild Activity Story

_____

_____

_____

_____

_____

_____

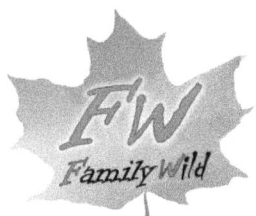
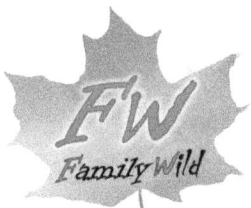

Animal Cleaning Station

Objective: Create a small cleaning station in a carefully identified part of your yard to make processing your animal harvest easier.

What You Might Need:

Two four-by-four timbers

One deck-quality two-by-four

Deck screws

Power drill

Saw

Plastic tub

Nylon cord, ¼ thickness.

Pebbles (optional)

Quick-set cement (optional)

Container to attach to finished frame to hold cleaning knife

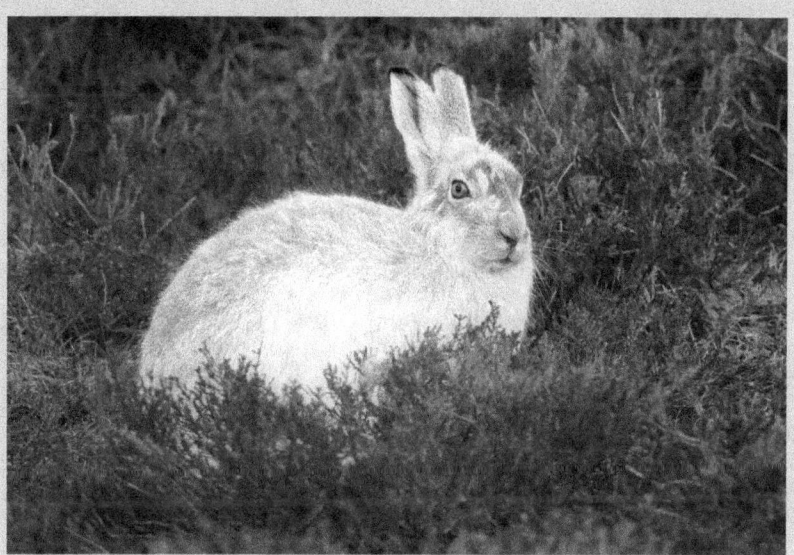

Jump in!

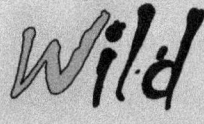

QUOTE

"Hunting, fishing, drawing, and music occupied my every moment. Cares I knew not, and cared naught about them."

John James Audubon

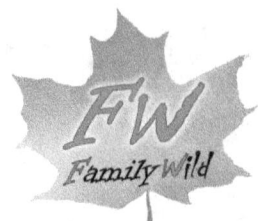

If you are planning to make a complete game cleaning station, please consider where you can also put the fish cleaning station as well-making both stations side by side can truly help you process your animal harvest with ease!

Select your spot-shade is nice in the hot summertime.

Dig your first hole 2. 5 feet down, then measure your second hole about six feet from the first. (This will give you room for your cross beam 2x4, with some nice overhang.

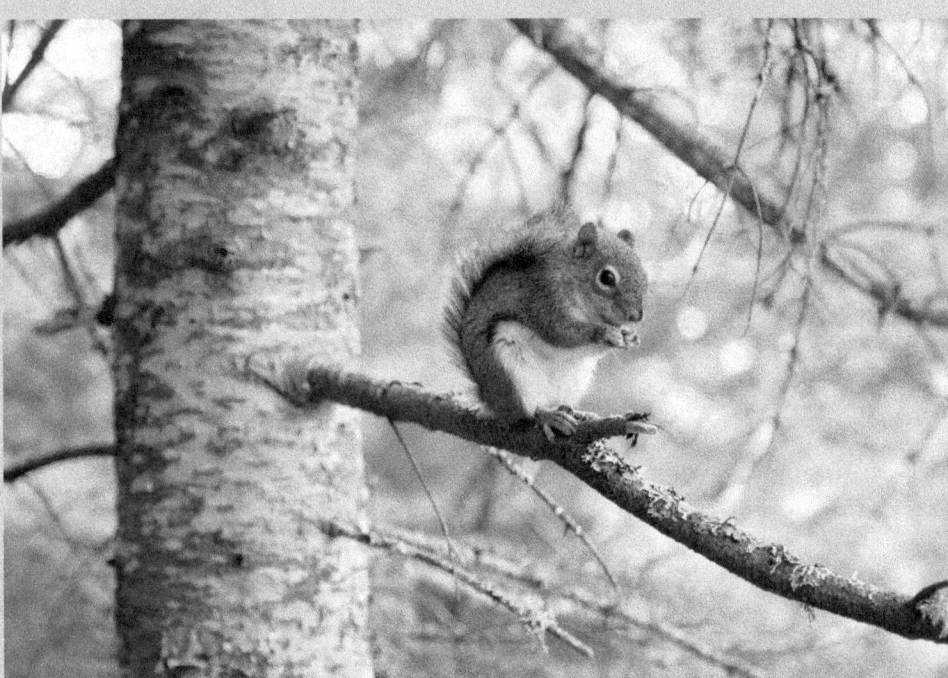

It's helpful to pour in some pebbles at the bottom of the hole to help "foot" the beam in very loose soil. Sometimes, it is best to pour some fast-set concrete to keep the beams steady.

Next, partially drill six screws into the 2x4, each set approximately six to ten inches apart. The screws should not be flush to the wood! These will be used to anchor a small piece of nylon rope.

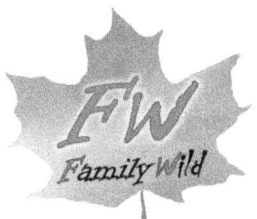

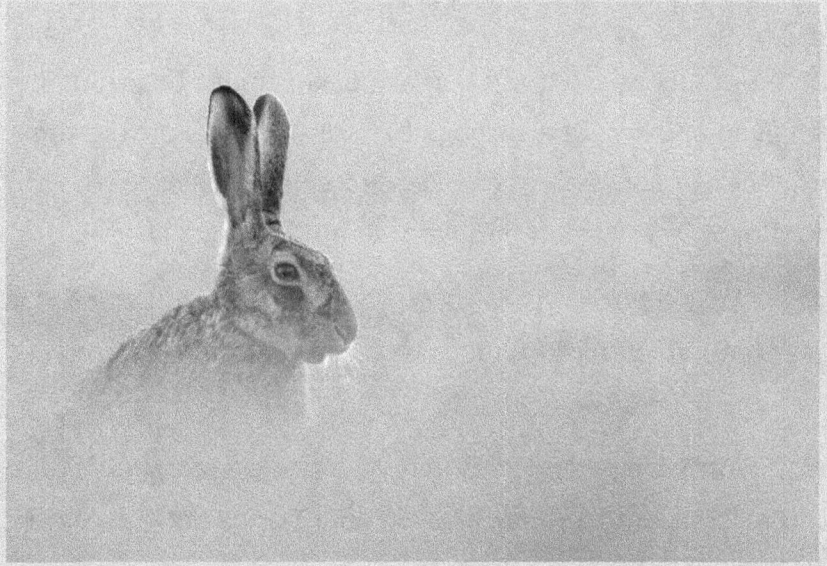

Tie a loop at one end of about one foot of nylon cord and snug up to the screw.

Once all the cord is in place, attach the 2x4 to the two 4x4 posts with decking screws.

If you decide to affix a small container to one of the 4x4's to hold your cleaning implements, be sure to drill small holes in the bottom.

Or use a terra cotta pot with a drain hole--you can add a few pebbles if the drain hole allows your knife to slip through. Simply use more cord or a piece of wire and attach the container to your cleaning station.

The hanging cords should be adjusted to fit your height-you can knot on more cord if you are on the short side like me! For cleaning rabbits, squirrels, even birds, you simply knot the cord around one leg, stretch open the animal and attach the other leg.

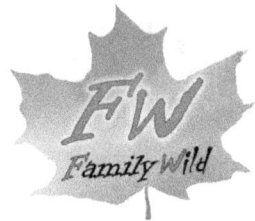

It's very helpful to put an easy to clean pan or bucket under the animal being cleaned-you can even line it with a garbage bag for disposal, or toss the remains to the chickens. (If you ever come across a diseased animal, be sure NOT to feed the leftovers to your flock. Discard all the meat at once!)

I've seen some folks add a hook on their 4x4 for a towel-as you want at your station, you may come up with more ideas to create a more functional environment.

It's very helpful if your fish cleaning station is nearby - you can finish processing your animal on the "countertop" and clean up your hands and implements easily.

In this age of antibiotics and growth hormones, hunting for some of the family meals is a smart way to live a little Wild - and healthier!

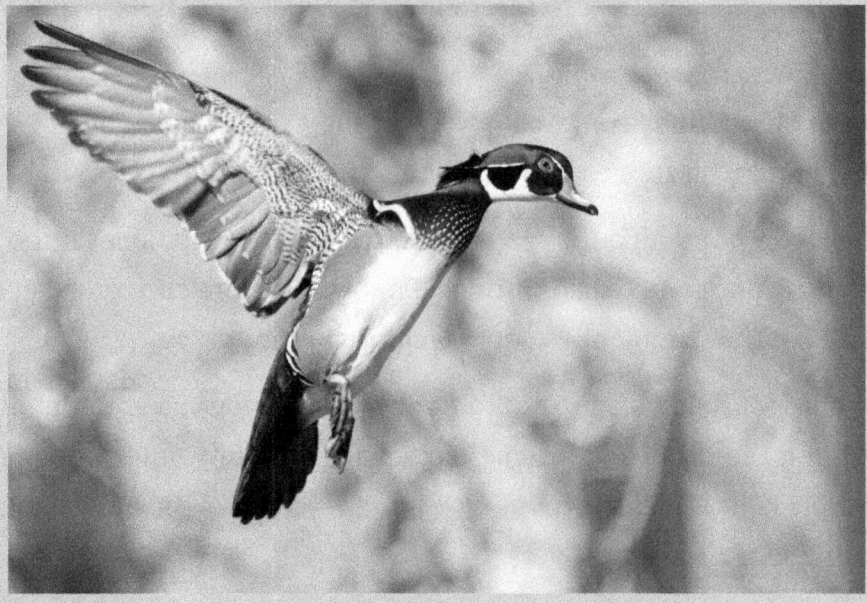

SCRAPBOOK PICTURES

Glue a couple pictures here
to remember your Activity

You can keep the pictures in Your Family Wild Activity book, your own Scrapbook, or put them in a frame to commemorate your activities years from now!

Below-take a few minutes and tell your ACTIVITY STORY.
In your own words. Think of it as telling the story to your Grandchildren some day! Do it in your own words and handwriting-like your sending a post card to someone 50-100 years from now!

Our Family Wild Activity Story

_____

_____

_____

_____

_____

_____

Family Wild

> "There are two primary choices in life: to accept conditions as they exist, or accept the responsibility for changing them."
>
> — Denis Waitley

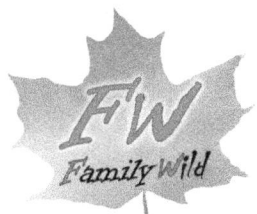
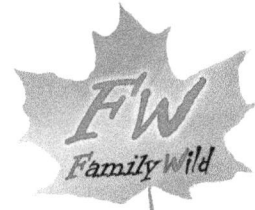

Fish Cleaning Station

Objective: Repurposing an old sink to create a small outdoor fish cleaning station.

What You Might Need:

An old sink from a place like Restore or Goodwill

A connection to an outside a water source

If you can't find a sink that is continuous with a counter top, you'll need to add a table or recycled counter top. A sink-metal counter top as one unit is the very best, because they are easy to clean and weather the elements much better than wood.

A hose to connect your sink to your water source

A drain pipe to run the blood and bits and pieces of flesh to a location you choose

Weather-resistant 4x4's to act as support legs

Additional deck grade lumber as needed

Four cement pavers to rest the feet of the 4x4's on

Deck screws

Level

Plumbing fixtures to attach both a faucet to your sink

Plumbing tape and orange and purple pipe cement as needed

Saw and power screw driver as needed.

Optional: Fish cleaning clamp and board, towel rack, ceramic or plastic container to hold fish cleaning implements

Jump in!

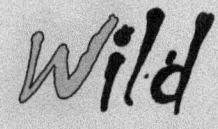

"We are cutting things kids like-music, art, and gym classes; stuff that kept me in school. This country can't survive without you kids. It's all about you kids."

Actor - Tony Danza

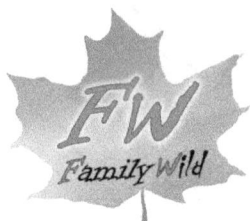

For this project, get to know your local Restore or Goodwill. Garage sales, Craig's List (online) or Facebook pages that feature local for-sale or giveaway items are also good bets for finding the materials you will need.

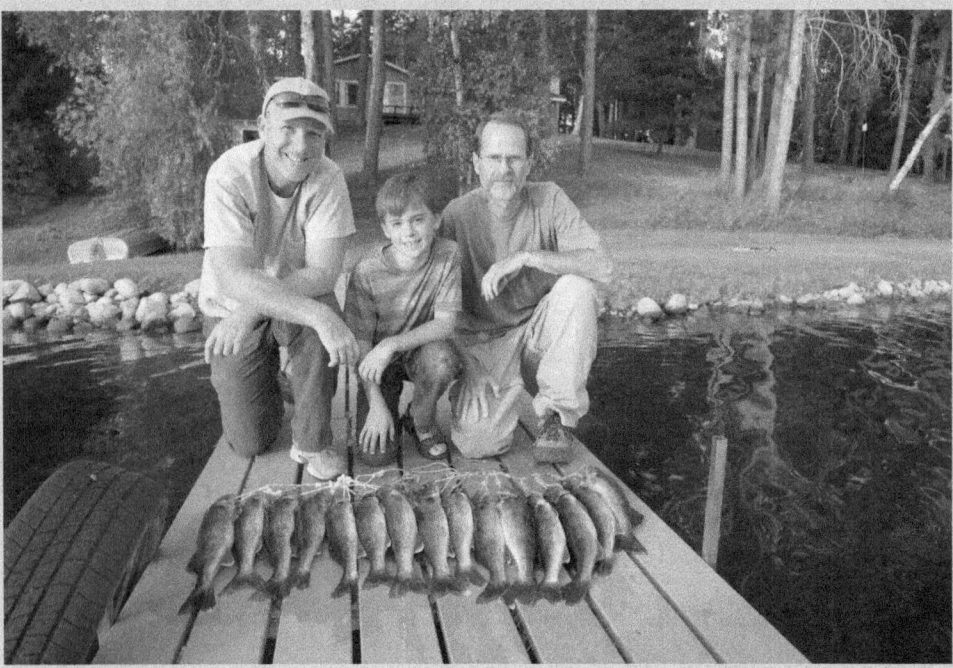

As we mentioned above, if you can find a metal sink that is continuous with a metal counter-top, grab it right away! The metal will weather well and be the easiest surface to clean.

First, identify where the station will be built. It must be within reach of a hose that attaches to the water source, and a site where you can link your drain pipe. I love running this clean-up water out to my chickens, who devour the small bits of fish that wash down the sink.

Try to keep the run off away from your gardens or play areas. Choose a space that is relatively level. Shade is nice in the hot summer time!

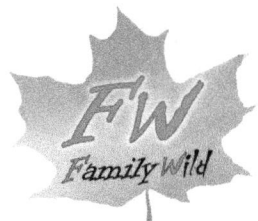

Cut your 4x4's to a height that is comfortable for you. Carefully measure the size of the sink and countertop, then connect the 4x4's with deck 2x4's--this will create the frame the sink and countertop will rest upon. It is helpful to put the foot of each 4x4 on a cement paver to help prevent rot in the wood. You can use a level to be sure you have a relatively flat surface through-out.

Place the countertop and sink on the frame you have created. Install your sink fixtures, hose connections and drain pipe. (Not sure how to do this? Grab your computer or smartphone and check out some of the You Tube tutorials! Or stroll into your local hardware store-employees there will usually walk you through the process.)

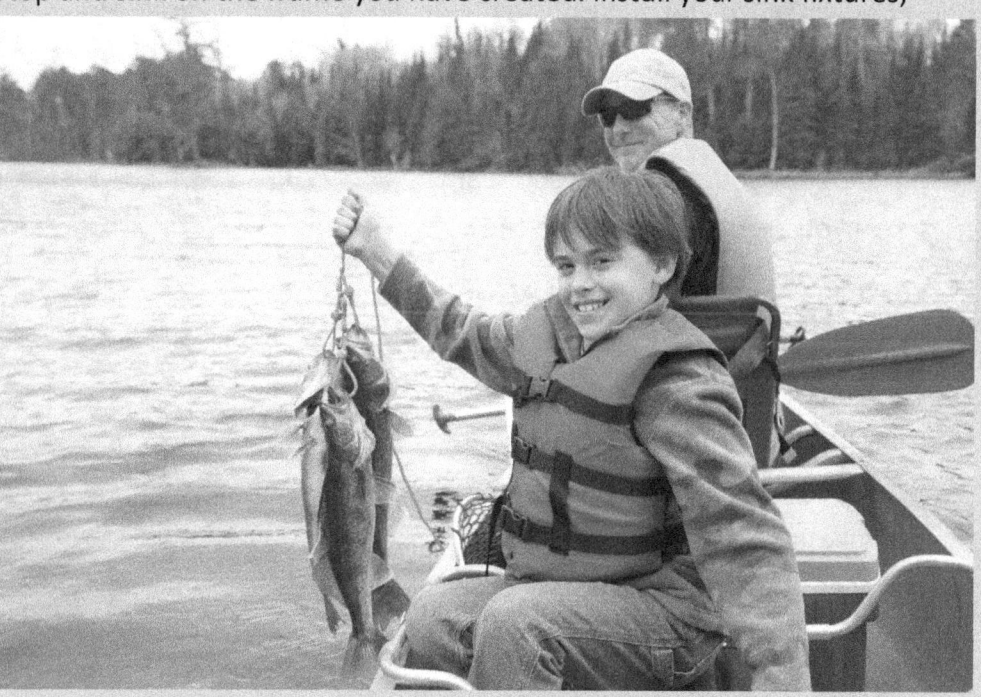

Luckily, it doesn't need to be perfect! (My husband plans on three trips to the hardware store when he does a plumbing project-but I reckon a little careful planning on your end may cut this down a bit! HA!)

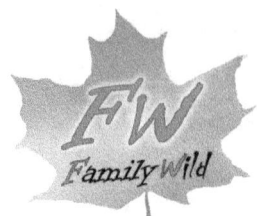

One additional fish cleaning item is very helpful: a board mounted with a clamp to help hold the fish steady. These can often be picked up at garage sales or resale shops, or can be bought new in most sporting goods departments and a stores. Think about hanging a towel rack on one end and keep a ceramic container on the station as a handy place to put your filet knife and scaler when you aren't working with them.

To clean your area, you want to avoid dumping chemicals on your property. Try a mix of white vinegar and water (one-part water to three-parts white vinegar). Damp a cloth or sponge with the mixture and wipe down all the surfaces. It cleans well and will break down naturally.

If you have set up a small game cleaning station nearby, the outdoor sink is a great place to finish butchering and cleaning your implements. It also can double as a nice work space for repotting garden plants.

Enjoy your Wild cleaning station! No more fish smells indoor and cleanup is easy!

SCRAPBOOK PICTURES

*Glue a couple pictures here
to remember your Activity*

You can keep the pictures in Your Family Wild Activity book,
your own Scrapbook, or put them in a frame
to commemorate your activities years from now!

Below-take a few minutes and tell your ACTIVITY STORY.
In your own words. Think of it as telling the story to
your Grandchildren some day! Do it in your own words
and handwriting-like your sending a post card to
someone 50-100 years from now!

Our Family Wild Activity Story

_____

_____

_____

_____

_____

_____

Family Wild

"The first track is the end of a string. At the far end, a being is moving; a mystery, dropping a hint about itself every so many feet, telling you more about itself until you can almost see it, even before you come to it.

The mystery reveals itself slowly, track by track, giving its genealogy early to coax you in. Further on, it will tell you the intimate details of its life and work, until you know the maker of the track like a lifelong friend."

(Tom Brown Jr., *The Tracker*)

Visit us at www.familywildprogram.com

Like us on Facebook at Family Wild

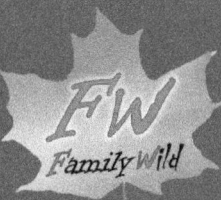

Family Wild

Chapter 4

Family Wild's Highest Honor

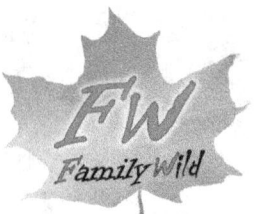 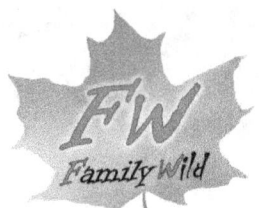

Teddy Roosevelt "Walk Softly" Circle of Honor

Family Wild's Highest Honor

According to the US National Park Service Webpage
https://www.nps.gov/thro/learn/historyculture/theodore-roosevelt-and-conservation.htm

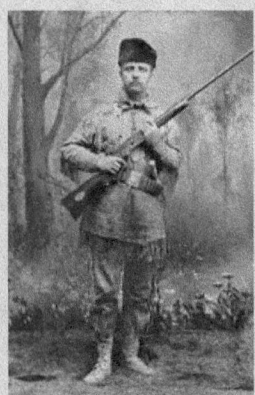

Theodore Roosevelt is often considered the "conservationist president." In the North Dakota Badlands, where many of his personal concerns first gave rise to his later environmental efforts, Roosevelt is remembered with a national park that bears his name and honors the memory of this great conservationist.

"We have fallen heirs to the most glorious heritage a people ever received, and each one must do his part if we wish to show that the nation is worthy of its good fortune."

Theodore "Teddy" Roosevelt
26th President of the United States

President Roosevelt challenged American's maintain the great natural resources of our lands. As a result, *Family Wild* honors President Roosevelt's hunting and conservation legacy with our HIGHEST HONOR.

To earn membership into the **Teddy Roosevelt "Walk Softly" Conservation Circle of Honor** your *Family Wild* club must do your part to improve the glorious heritage of our North American lands. Although we all can't be President of the United States or the Canadian Prime Minister, everyone of us can make our environment better than we found it.

Wild Quote

"I recognize the right and duty of this generation to develop and use the natural resources of our land; but I do not recognize the right to waste them, or to rob, by wasteful use, the generations that come after us.

Theodore "Teddy" Roosevelt-26th President

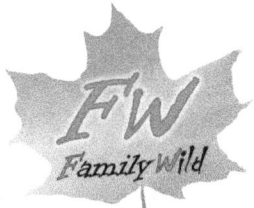 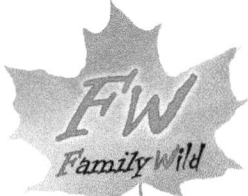

Teddy Roosevelt
"Walk Softly"
Circle of Honor

The National Park Service Website continues-

The decimation of bison, and the eradication of elk, bighorn sheep, deer and other game species was a loss which Roosevelt felt indicative of society's perception of our natural resources. He saw the effects of overgrazing, and suffered the <u>loss of his ranches</u> because of it. While many still considered natural resources inexhaustible, Roosevelt would write:

"We have become great because of the lavish use of our resources. But the time has come to inquire seriously what will happen when our forests are gone, when the coal, the iron, the oil, and the gas are exhausted, when the soils have still further impoverished and washed into the streams, polluting the rivers, denuding the fields and obstructing navigation."

Theodore "Teddy" Roosevelt
26th President of the United States

Conservation increasingly became one of Roosevelt's main concerns. After becoming President in 1901, Roosevelt used his authority to protect wildlife and public lands by creating the United States Forest Service (USFS) and establishing 150 national forests, 51 federal bird reserves, 4 national game preserves, 5 national parks, and 18 national monuments by enabling the <u>1906 American Antiquities Act</u>. During his presidency, Theodore Roosevelt protected approximately 230 million acres of public land.

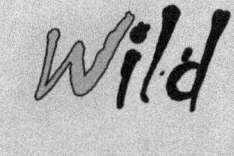

"Of all the questions which can come before this nation, short of the actual preservation of its existence in a great war, there is none which compares in importance with the great central task of leaving this land even a better land for our descendants than it is for us."

Theodore "Teddy" Roosevelt -26th President

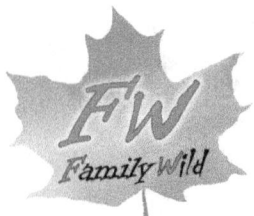
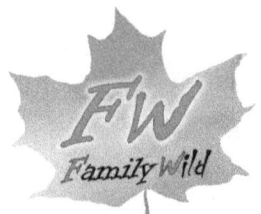

Teddy Roosevelt "Walk Softly" Circle of Honor

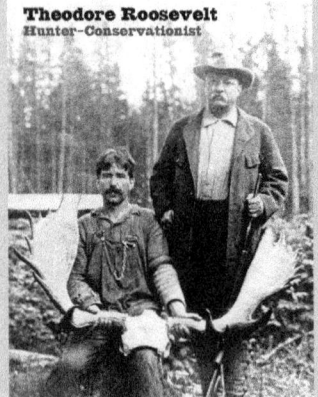

Please understand, we expect all **Family Wild** clubs and members to leave our environment better than you found it. If you find garbage in the woods, pick it up and dispose of it properly. If you find trash floating in a lake, river or stream grab it and throw it out.

However, to enter the exclusive **Family Wild's** Highest Honor-the **Teddy Roosevelt "Walk Softly" Circle of Honor** - your club must complete a project that improves the environment to a substantial level.

You will need to capture "before" pictures/video of your project area, showing us the condition of the environment you want to improve. You need to document your project through photos and videos illustrating the efforts of your members to "Walk Softly and Carry a Big Stick" to pursue your groups environmental improvements.

You will need to document a minimum of 80 club hours on your project. The documentation needs to reflect each members documented contribution to your team's efforts.

You will need to document the daily progress of your project-indicating the "high" and the "lows" as you move along. Keep in mind, you're setting the stage for others to replicate your project. As a result, make sure you indicate what worked and what didn't, so others can benefit from your experience.

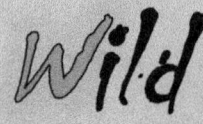

QUOTE

"There are no words that can tell the hidden spirit of the wilderness, that can reveal its mystery, its melancholy and its charm."

Theodore "Teddy" Roosevelt - 26th President

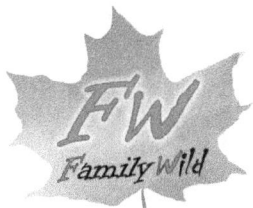
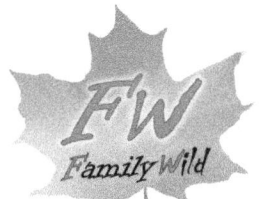

Teddy Roosevelt
"Walk Softly"
Circle of Honor

Family Wild's
Highest Honor

In as much as Teddy Roosevelt made famous the term "Bully Pulpit," using bully meant "superb" or "wonderful," and that the White House afforded him the platform to announce to the world his thoughts and visions.

As a result, in the memory of President Roosevelt, you need to let the world know your

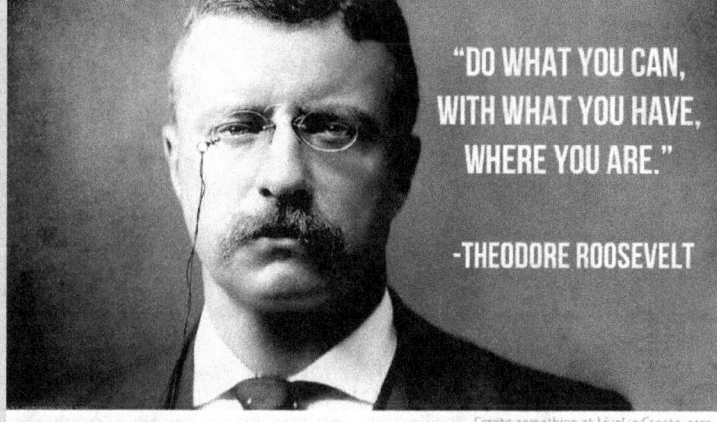

accomplishments. You'll need to document your press releases, press conference and retain any publications, radio and television news broadcasts. Don't be shy-someone in your club can answer questions from the media to celebrate your family's accomplishment.

We understand that many folks don't like to toot their own horn. However, by publicly announcing your efforts you set the example for others to follow with projects of their own.

Wild QUOTE

The farther one gets into the wilderness, the greater is the attraction of its lonely freedom."

Theodore "Teddy" Roosevelt -26th President

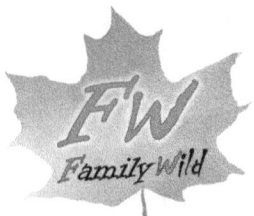
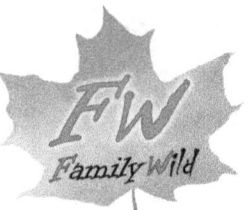

Teddy Roosevelt
"Walk Softly"
Circle of Honor

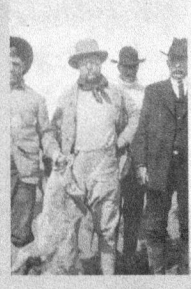
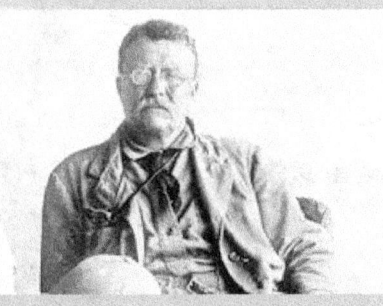
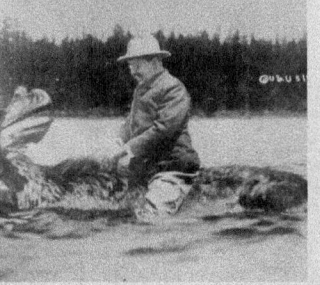

We ask that you work with your children to submit a 1000-2000 word essay on your project. We want you to document the following themes:

Where did your idea originate? What materials did you use?

Who helped and their relationship in the family and ages. How long did your project take?

Describe the highlight moment of your project.

What would you do differently. **Who will your project benefit? Explain.**

Did you partner with others? Did others donate time, materials? If so, who and what?

What future efforts will you need to do to maintain your project?

What did you do to promote your projects results?

How were the results and what would you do differently?

Wild QUOTE

"There are no words that can tell the hidden spirit of the wilderness, that can reveal its mystery, its melancholy and its charm."

Theodore "Teddy" Roosevelt - 26th President

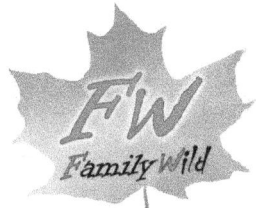
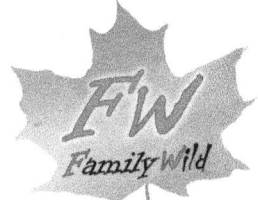

Teddy Roosevelt
"Walk Softly"
Circle of Honor

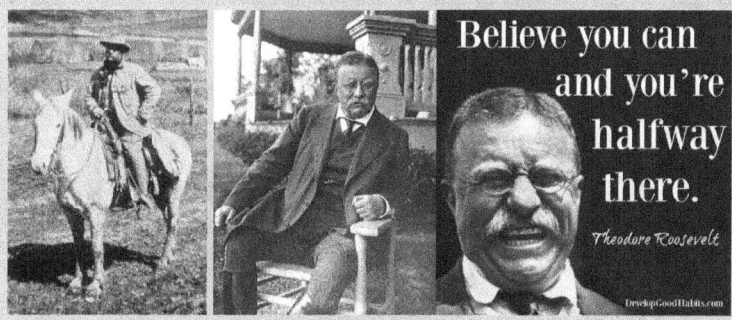

We also ask that you work with your children to submit a 500 word essay on President Teddy Roosevelt. For your topic, pick a Roosevelt quote or historical fact you found interesting.

Please convey the quote or fact, when it occurred, and where it occurred. Describe why your group chose that quote or fact and what it meant to you in relation to your project.

Explain the impact President Roosevelt played in the sport of hunting, conservation, and/or the National Park System.

So often we don't take time to remember our history and those who impacted the natural resources we enjoy today. The original premise of **Family Wild** was to bring children together with parents together with grandparents to make time to pass on life experiences from one generation to the next.

Enjoy learning about one of America's most intriguing President's and the Father of American Conservation -Teddy Roosevelt.

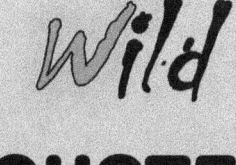

"Now and then we hear the wilder voices of the wilderness, from animals that in the hours of darkness do not fear the neighborhood of man: the coyotes wail like dismal ventriloquists, or the silence may be broken by the snorting and stamping of a deer."

Theodore "Teddy" Roosevelt - 26th President

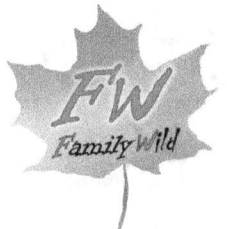 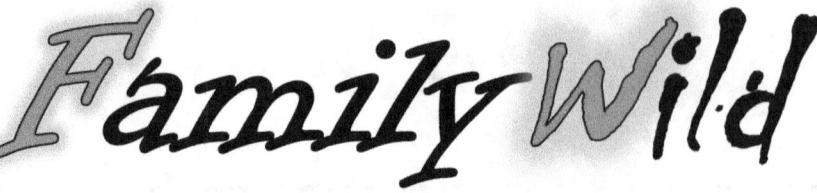 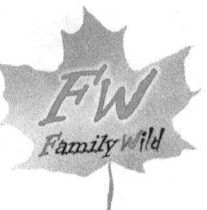

Teddy Roosevelt
"Walk Softly"
Circle of Honor
Application

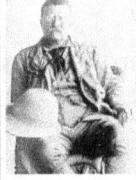 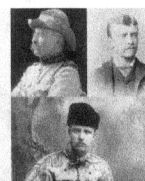 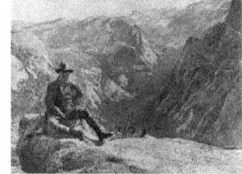

Application Date-_____

Family Wild Group Name _____

Group Contact Person-_____

Address _____ _____ _____
                      Street Address   State Zip Code

Contact Phone Number _____

Contact E-Mail _____

Items Needed for Application:

Before Pictures _____   **During Pictures** _____

After Pictures _____   **Press Documents** _____

Volunteer Hours Report _____   **Project Essays** _____

_____   _____

Contact Signature   Contact Printed Name

SCRAPBOOK PICTURES

Glue a couple pictures here
to remember your Activity

You can keep the pictures in Your Family Wild Activity book, your own Scrapbook, or put them in a frame to commemorate your activities years from now!

Below-take a few minutes and tell your ACTIVITY STORY. In your own words. Think of it as telling the story to your Grandchildren some day! Do it in your own words and handwriting-like your sending a post card to someone 50-100 years from now!

Our Family Wild Activity Story

_____

_____

_____

_____

_____

_____

SCRAPBOOK PICTURES

Glue a couple pictures here to remember your Activity

You can keep the pictures in Your Family Wild Activity book, your own Scrapbook, or put them in a frame to commemorate your activities years from now!

Below-take a few minutes and tell your ACTIVITY STORY. In your own words. Think of it as telling the story to your Grandchildren some day! Do it in your own words and handwriting-like your sending a post card to someone 50-100 years from now!

Our Family Wild Activity Story

_____

_____

_____

_____

_____

_____

_____

Family Wild

Appendix

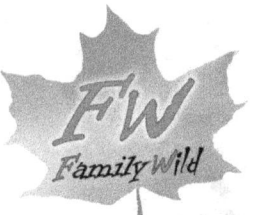
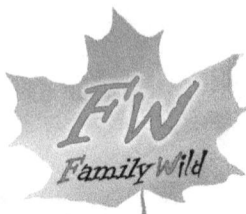

Family Wild

More Cool Stuff

I. Adult Photo Release Example

II. Child Photo Release Example

III. Intellectual Property Release

IV. Family Wild Activity Form

V. Family Wild Vision Statement

VI. Family Wild Mission Statement

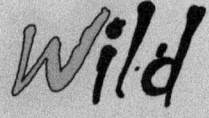
QUOTE

"Immerse yourself in the outdoor experience. It will cleanse your soul and make you a better person."

Archer - Fred Bear

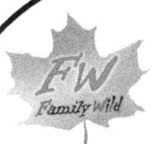 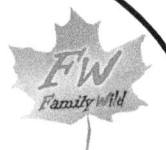

Family Wild

Adult Photo Release

I hereby authorize **Family Wild** Alpena Chapter hereafter referred to as the "Company" to publish photographs taken of me on August 15 2016 and my name and likeness, for use in the **Family Wild** Alpena Chapters print, online and video-based marketing materials, press releases, as well as any other Company publications.

I hereby release and hold harmless **Family Wild** Alpena Chapter from any reasonable expectation of privacy or confidentiality associated with the images specified above.

I further acknowledge that my voluntary participation and that I will not receive financial compensation of any type associated with the taking or publications of these photographs or participation in company marketing materials or other Company publications. I acknowledge and agree that publications of said photos confers no rights of ownership or royalties whatsoever.

I hereby release **Family Wild** Alpena Chapter, its contractors, its employees and any third parties involved in the creation or publication of marketing materials, from liability for any claims by me or any third party in connection with my participation.

Authorization: Printed Name _____

                               Signature _____

                               Address_____

Feel free to use this sample Photo Release form or check with your own attorney for their recommendations. We live in a sue-happy society. DON'T take for granted that everyone wants their picture published. Cover all your bases and your backside and have everyone fill out this form as part of REGISTRATION. That way, you'll know **before** you take pictures/video and publicize them who wants DOESN'T want to see themselves in the paper, on the news or on your website. As a former professional photographer, I know you want this form as part of your registration packet! **BETTER SAFE THAN SORRY!**

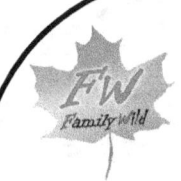
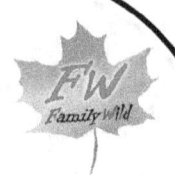

Family Wild

Adult/Minor Child Photo Release

I hereby authorize Family Wild Alpena Chapter hereafter referred to as the "Company" to publish photographs taken of me on October August and likenesses, for use in the Family Wild Alpena Chapters print, online and video-based marketing materials, press releases, as well as any other Company publications.

I hereby release and hold harmless Family Wild Alpena Chapter from any reasonable expectation of privacy or confidentiality of myself and my minor children associated with the images specified above. Further, I attest that I am the parent or legal guardian of the child or children listed below and that I have full authority to consent and authorize Family Wild Alpena Chapter to use their likeness and names.

I further acknowledge that my voluntary participation and that I, the minor child or children, will not receive financial compensation of any type associated with the taking or publications of these photographs or participation in company marketing materials or other Company publications. I acknowledge and agree that publications of said photos confers no rights of ownership or royalties whatsoever.

I hereby release Family Wild Alpena Chapter, its contractors, its employees and any third parties involved in the creation or publication of marketing materials, from liability for any claims by me or any third party in connection with my participation or the minor children listed below.

Authorization: Printed Name _____

                              Signature _____

                              Address _____

Names and Ages of Minor Children

                              Name_____ Age _____

                              Name_____ Age _____

Feel free to use this sample Minor Child Photo Release form or check with your own attorney for their recommendations. Have every parent/guardian fill this out at registration. **AGAIN - BETTER SAFE THAN SORRY.**

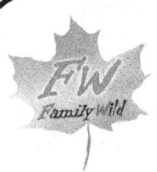

Intellectual Property Release Form

INTELLECTUAL PROPERTY RELEASE FORM - I authorize **Family Wild, LLC** to use copyright materials, images, recordings, names or personal information of the following: _____ the undersigned, understand that I own the copyright on any materials I've provided to **Family Wild, LLC,** and I can, if I so wish, grant permission to others the right to publish materials I produce. I, therefore, do hereby grant to: **Family Wild, LLC,** its successors, and assigns, the absolute unlimited right to use and/or publish photographs, video, print, electronic or any other media, or intellectual property, the following materials as originally produced unless a written agreement detailing any changes to the materials is obtained between me and **Family Wild, LLC** to which I am providing consent.

Attached to this consent form are the original materials to which I am providing consent to use and any written agreement regarding changes to the original materials. **(Description of materials attached to this form)** I hereby warrant I am the author/owner/publisher of the materials I am providing and/or that I have obtained all necessary legal rights and permissions to use the materials and/or convey their use to others. The permission I have obtained and assigned to above-named organization is limited to using the materials as originally produced unless a written agreement is obtained between me and the above-named organization to alter the materials and in which all changes to the original materials will be noted.

I hereby warrant that I am of full legal age and have the right to contract in my own name. I have read the above authorization, release and agreement prior to its execution, am fully familiar with and understand the contents thereof, and agree to its terms knowingly and voluntarily. This consent and release shall be binding upon me and my heirs, legal representatives, and assigns.

_____   _____
(Print Name)   Signature

Date _____

Vision Statement

Visit us at www.familywild.com

Like us on Facebook at Family Wild

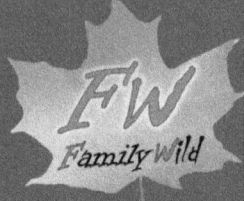

Family Wild

Bringing Generations together celebrating Family, Friendship, and Fun.

Mission Statement

Visit us at www.familywildprogram.com

Like us on Facebook at Family Wild

Family Wild

Family Wild

strives to pass

on the historic

North American outdoor

experience while creating fun opportunities,

activities, events and forums bringing

generations together in family group

celebrations of each other and

the great outdoors.

Visit us at www.familywild.com

Like us on Facebook at Family Wild

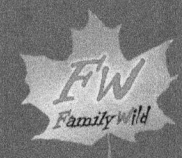

Family Wild

Visit our online storefront at

www.familywildprogram.com

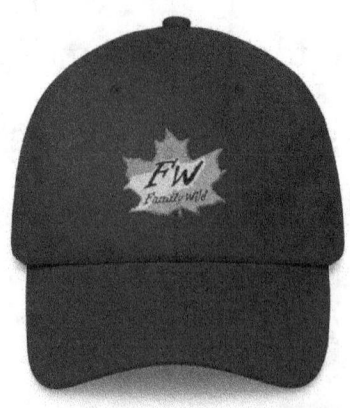

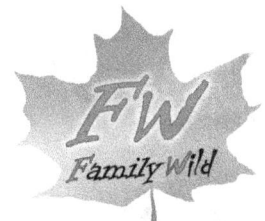

About the Author

Kim Nunneley holds a master's degree in comparative religion and a graduate certificate in holistic healthcare from Western Michigan University. She studied adult spiritual formation at the Iliff School of Theology in Denver, Colorado.

Living on 50 acres of cedar in Northern Michigan, she and her husband work at improving their hunting lands, garden and raise chickens, rabbits and goats. Kim has written over twenty books, ranging from science fiction to poetry to comparative religion titles.

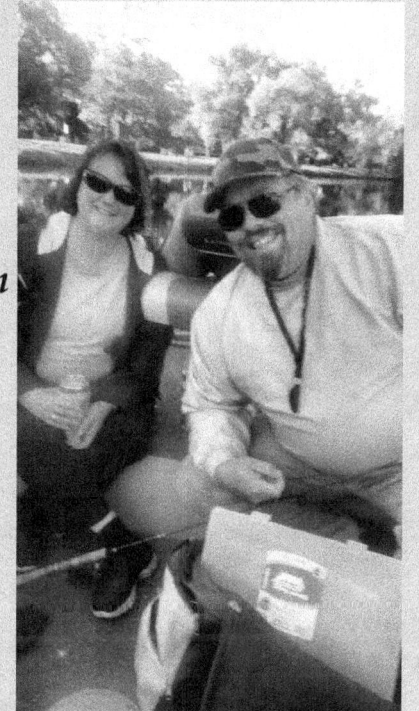

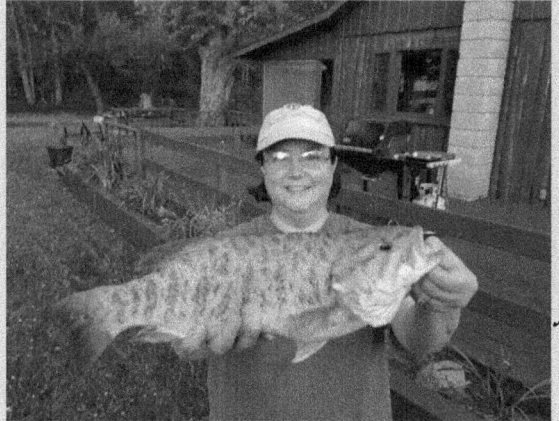

You can read her blog at http://guhacaveoftheheart.blogspot.com

Your Black & White Family Wild

Arts Activities
Volume I

Strengthening Family Through Nature - based Creativity

Kim Nunneley